The Yale Ben Jonson

GENERAL EDITORS: ALVIN B. KERNAN AND RICHARD B. YOUNG

Ben Jonson: Epicoene

EDITED BY EDWARD PARTRIDGE

NEW HAVEN AND LONDON:

YALE UNIVERSITY PRESS, 1971

Copyright © 1971 by Yale University.
All rights reserved. This book may not be
reproduced, in whole or in part, in any form
(except by reviewers for the public press),
without written permission from the publishers.
Library of Congress catalog card number: 70–151577
International standard book number: 0–300–01411–2

Set in Aldine Bembo type by Clowes,
and printed in the United States of America by
The Murray Printing Co., Forge Village, Mass.

Distributed in Great Britain, Europe, and Africa by
Yale University Press, Ltd., London; in Canada by
McGill-Queen's University Press, Montreal; in Australasia by
Australia and New Zealand Book Co., Pty., Ltd.,
Artarmon, New South Wales; in India by UBS Publishers'
Distributors Pvt., Ltd., Delhi; in Japan by John
Weatherhill, Inc., Tokyo.

To Viola

Contents

Preface of the General Editors

The Yale edition of the plays of Ben Jonson is intended to meet two fundamental requirements: first, the need of the modern reader for a readily intelligible text which will convey, as nearly as an edition can, the life and movement which invests the plays on the stage; second, the need of the critic and scholar for a readily available text which represents as accurately as possible, though it does not reproduce, the plays as Jonson printed them. These two requirements are not, we believe, incompatible, but the actual adjustment of one to the other has been determined by the judgment of the individual editors. In details of editorial practice, therefore, the individual volumes of the edition may vary, but in basic editorial principle they are consistent.

The texts are based primarily on the two folio volumes of Jonson's *Works*, the first published in 1616, the second in 1640. The 1616 volume was seen through the press by Jonson himself, and therefore represents to a degree unusual for dramatic texts of the period what the dramatist intended us to have. The 1640 volume presents more difficult textual problems; though Jonson himself began preparing individual plays for it as early as 1631, these were carelessly printed—a fact of which he was painfully aware—and the folio, under the editorship of the eccentric Sir Kenelm Digby, was not completed until after Jonson's death. The quarto editions have also been consulted, and where a quarto reading has been preferred by an editor the necessary information appears in the notes.

In editing Jonson for the modern reader, one of the central problems is that of annotation, a problem that is complicated rather than solved by providing a catalogue of Jonson's immense classical learning or of his contemporary lore. We·have believed that annotation is most helpful not when it identifies or defines details but when it clarifies the context of the detail. Consequently, citation of sources, allusions, and analogues, whether classical or colloquial, has been controlled by and restricted to what is relevant in the judgment of the editors to a meaningful understanding of the dramatic and poetic values of the passage in question and of the play as a whole. For the same reason, all editorial apparatus—introductions, notes, and glosses—frequently and deliberately deal with critical and interpretative matters in order to reanimate the topical details and give substance to the imaginative world each play creates.

Where Jonson printed all verse in the metrical unit of the line, whether or not it represents the speech of one or more than one character, this edition divides the parts of such lines according to the speaker, and indicates the metrical unit by echeloning the parts of the line.

The original punctuation has been followed where its rhetorical effect has a dramatic value, but modern pointing has been used wherever necessary to clarify syntactical obscurities and to eliminate obvious errors or mere eccentricity. Spelling has been modernized except where orthographical change affects either meaning or meter. For example, where Jonson prints *'d* to indicate an unstressed ending of a past participle, this edition prints *-ed*, and where Jonson printed *-ed* to indicate stress this edition prints *-èd*. Jonson's frequent elisions, e.g. *th'* or *i'*, are retained, and all unusual accents are marked.

Introduction

Epicoene is uniquely Jonson's, yet unique even for Jonson. He left his signature on its coherent design, its unrelenting irony, the variety of its comic motifs, and the decorum of its speech and action. No one else could have written it, and not even Jonson wrote another quite like it. In no other comedy did he confine the events so strictly to the life of the minor gentry of contemporary London or the sound and rhythm of the dialogue so largely to its colloquial speech; and in no other comedy did he achieve a tone so bright and gay (whatever the darker notes sounded by Morose's surly humor and its castigation).

This gay tone, the lilt and graceful energy of the dialogue, and the special focus on young men-about-town strike us immediately in the first scene. This scene, like the whole first act, moves with such an air of casual improvisation that one is likely to overlook the careful art Jonson brought to it, his masterful creation of the cool distance and amused detachment which ironic comedy requires. What could be more normal—dressing, singing, talking with friends who drop in, criticizing women? And the topics seem topical enough—the use of cosmetics, the wasting of time, trouble with relatives, a search for a wife, an invitation to dinner. Only gradually does it become clear that Jonson, with relaxed ease, has introduced, sometimes quite obliquely, motifs which are crucial to later scenes. Such apparently incongruous subjects as cosmetics, the Collegiates, an uncle who

I

disinherits a nephew, a suitor who searches for a dumb wife, a fool like La Foole, or a lover like Daw are in fact seen as variations on the great Renaissance themes of art and nature.

A good share of our enjoyment of these variations comes from the extraordinary art with which Jonson wittily relates them or judiciously distinguishes them in an action that moves with seemingly careless ease. The dramatic devices which constitute that action —exposure and revelation, descriptions of foolish behavior, baiting and deception, anticipations and ironic reversals—not only serve as formal motifs for the scenic structure but also express and explore the central theme. Although the motifs are varied constantly, a number of general patterns can be discerned.

Exposure is plainly crucial to both the action and the meaning of *Epicoene*, and since self-exposure is more complete, more ridiculous, and essentially more comic than description, it usually precedes or replaces exposure by others. A character's folly may be sketched in just before he enters (both La Foole and Daw are described in I.3, and one is first seen in I.4, the other not until III.3), but even when his weakness is exposed by the manipulation of other characters, the scene is overheard and observed by still others. Such overhearing is dramatically useful not merely because it increases the social pressure involved in the exposure but also because it affords the playwright another perspective for comment. Exposures by the manipulation of others increase in number and moral seriousness as the play moves toward its resolution; in act IV there are four separate instances of overhearing.

On the other hand, descriptions of comic behavior are, understandably enough, more frequent in the first two acts than in the last three. They are chiefly useful in whetting our interest in characters before they appear or in preparing us to perceive their self-exposure when they are on stage. But Act III contains a brilliant variation of this device in Morose's description, here optative rather than preparatory, of Cutbeard's fate as a renegade barber. And the dismissals of Morose, Daw, and La Foole might be considered the final examples of this device.

Baiting, like manipulated exposure, increases in frequency and intensity throughout the play. In the first two acts Clerimont and Dauphine almost casually tease the dunces, La Foole and Daw, and Truewit's torment of the egoistic Morose is largely improvised. But in the final three acts such torments as the shrewish Epicoene, noise of various kinds in increasing volume, the artificially manufactured quarrel between Daw and La Foole, and the final racking of Morose over divorce are increasingly more deliberate and intense.

The torments, like the exposures, are manipulated by the young against the old, the wits against the fools, the cheerful against the cheerless. Indeed, we anticipate them until the very end of the play. Surely one of the proofs of Jonson's extraordinary skill comes in the way he draws us, as he draws the witty young men, to successively more comic exposures and baitings. Dryden considered the intrigue of *Epicoene* "the greatest and most noble of any pure unmixed comedy in any language" in part because the business of the plot "rises" in every act.[1] Both the first two acts end with major characters leaving to see someone's folly exposed or discomfiture mocked. Act IV intensifies this exposure and mockery, almost from scene to scene, into a complex pattern of three separate exposures— of the Collegiates, Morose, and Daw and La Foole—all of which are completed only in the last act. Even the final revelation that Epicoene is a boy belongs to this pattern: if one is ignorant of Epicoene's sex, one has the explosive enjoyment of surprise at Dauphine's unmasking; but once one can anticipate the revelation, the final scene exploits the more mature pleasure of expectation to create the ironic joy of seeing someone else discover what one already knows.

---

1. "Essay of Dramatic Poesy," *Essays of John Dryden*, ed. W. P. Ker (New York, 1961), 1: 83, 88.

A similar joy in part accounts for our possibly malicious delight in ironic reversals. In *Epicoene* at least one peripety appears in every act except the first (and even there La Foole's self-exposure may turn back on itself, since his very attempt to impress Clerimont and Dauphine succeeds, but the reverse of the way intended). When the agent of discovery is the victim himself, witlessly unaware of how completely he is revealing himself, his self-exposure illustrates that reciprocal relationship of *anagnorisis* and *peripeteia* which Aristotle found characteristic of the most pleasingly complex of plots. Like the exposures and the baitings, such reversals increase in intensity as the play moves closer to its resolution. Truewit's baiting of Morose doubles back on itself. Morose, who marries chiefly to disinherit a nephew, is properly rewarded by getting a shrewish wife in place of a silent woman and by becoming a ward of the nephew. The knights, Daw and La Foole, prove cowardly where they ought to have been brave and boast of sleeping with a woman who turns out to be a boy. Finally, in the revelation of the real nature of Epicoene, everyone's knowledge of the truth, except Dauphine's, is shown to be defective, and only Truewit is not rendered speechless by the reversal. Few plays, excluding others by Jonson, control and vary an audience's great enjoyment of comic irony the way *Epicoene* does.

Even Truewit himself, though the very spirit of improvised gaiety, suffers from a continuous peripety. When he tries to break up the proposed marriage of Morose and Epicoene, the very extravagance of his effort to depict the miseries of marriage convinces Morose that he is working on Dauphine's behalf and brings about the marriage he sought to prevent. His reward at first is Clerimont's caustic appraisal—"Ignorantly officious, do services, and not know his why"—but the action turns back on his critics when they hear that Morose is going to marry Epicoene, as Dauphine wanted. Truewit exposes the cowardice of Daw and La Foole only to have their folly shift to boasting about lying with Epicoene. He makes the Collegiates all fall in love with Dauphine—to that gentleman's consternation. He arranges and conducts a mock-hearing on the question of divorce for a man who is not married at all. He ends by illustrating his own comment on Daw: "he that thinks himself the master-wit is the master fool" (III.6.45–46). His inventive improvising is ironically contrasted with the calculations of Dauphine, who has brought up Epicoene "this half year, at my great charges." But Truewit has good nature enough not to be resentful of Dauphine's secrecy, and quick wit enough to regain his voluble mastery over even so reversed a situation. Jonson's control of his characters is nowhere better illustrated than in his rendering of Truewit as wittily charming, maliciously inventive, but, because he is most ignorant where he is most sure, vain and ironically ludicrous.

Truewit's central function may be to keep a series of actions which might seem mordantly bitter gay, at times even lighthearted. Only this figure of nonchalance, drawn as close as Jonson could come to Castiglione's *sprezzatura*, keeps the play as aerial as it is in its apparently unpremeditated gaiety. That he and Clerimont usually improvise their torment makes them less malicious than the calculating Dauphine and more usable as comic manipulators than Dauphine is. And Truewit's gaiety, more than any other element in the play, makes it, as a Frenchman, Maurice Castelain, reminds the modern Englishman, Jonson's most joyous comedy.[2]

"Joyous" may seem a strange word for a play involving so much baiting and so many exposures. Perhaps only a Frenchman, brought up in a comic tradition that has not become so sentimental as that of the English, could see the joyousness of such a "comedy of affliction" (II.6.35). Most of us must use whatever imagination we can muster to understand comedy like Jonson's, whose harsh, at times homeopathic mood has not been present in English comedy since the plays of Congreve. The seventeenth century was still the age of

2. *Ben Jonson: L'Homme et L'Oeuvre* (Paris, 1907), p. 522.

the stocks and the pillory, the age in which idiots were publicly displayed, criminals publicly executed, and witches publicly burned, whereas contemporary civilization likes to tranquilize itself and soften the harsh edges of life. But if we bear in mind that the targets of Jonson's comic criticism are egotism and selfishness and vanity, it may help us to adopt, in our esthetic attitude, some of the Jacobean's toughmindedness toward the various kinds of folly and joylessness by which egotism is expressed. We must prevent ourselves from reading into the artificial comedies of the seventeenth century our own interest in the causes of human behavior and from confusing their stylized characters with actual human beings who may properly win our sympathies. The pure idiocy of Daw's "I would be loth to lose my right arm, for writing madrigals" (IV.5.109–10), when confronted with the necessity of pacifying La Foole, makes such confusion comic in itself. Nevertheless, we need not feel forced, I trust, to adopt the civic callousness of the age to acquire a rational judgment of its art. We are not, after all, members of a new and different race. Indeed, the enlightened psychology which presumably shows us more humane as well as more scientific than seventeenth-century Englishmen has revealed possibilities of moral confusion and moral indifference that might well have impressed Jonson, though they would not have surprised him.

If comedy of affliction forces us to find some cause in nature for hard hearts, we might approach it more naturally if we simply admitted what seems to me a fact, that some of our pleasure in such comedies results precisely from the exultant gamesmanship of its heroes, who anticipate, with delight, the discomfiture of their victims and describe, with relish, the ridiculous behavior of their favorite fools. To conclude, as R. G. Collingwood does, that "the Elizabethan was by temperament a bully" and that "in Shakespeare and his contemporaries, bullying in its most violent form is so common that we can only suppose the average playgoer to have conceived it as the salt of life" may be convenient but is not convincing. He comes closer to the truth when he says that "malice, the desire that others, especially those better than ourselves, should suffer, is a perpetual source of pleasure to man."[3] A source of pleasure to *all* men: from classical antiquity to the present the assertion has been made—by Plato, by Hobbes, by Bergson, by Freud—that our laughter at those whose discomfiture allows us to consider fools or knaves is an expression of our own malicious and aggressive impulses.

An explanation of laughter, however, does not explain literature; what makes us laugh does not necessarily make a work of art. It was, in fact, an opinion widely held in the Renaissance that laughter and comedy have at best no more than an accidental relationship, and though his own best work contradicts him, Jonson records with apparent approval the assertion, attributed to Aristotle, that "the moving of laughter is a fault in Comedie."[4] Ten years before writing *Epicoene* he had Cordatus, the "Moderator," in *Every Man Out of His Humor* ("The Authors friend; A man inly acquainted with the scope and drift of his Plot: Of a discreet, and understanding judgement"), advise the critic that until he can do better he "content himselfe with CICEROS definition"—that comedy is the imitation of life, the mirror of custom, the image of truth— "*Imitatio vitae, Speculum consuetudinis, Imago veritatis*; a thing throughout pleasant, and ridiculous, and accommodated to the correction of manners" (*H & S*, 3: 515). The series of paired but opposing terms, elaborations of "the imitation of what is natural," are in fact versions of "art" and "nature," the terms which are basic to the play. What Jonson meant by "art" and "nature" and how he related them are matters central to the technique as well as the meaning of his comedy.

---

3. Collingwood, *The Principles of Art* (Oxford, 1938), p. 87.

4. C. H. Herford and Percy and Evelyn Simpson, eds., *Ben Jonson* (Oxford, 1925–52), 8: 643. Hereafter cited as *H & S*.

As the emphasis on "customs" and "manners" suggests, the "imitation of what is natural" is concerned with human nature as it expresses itself in society. The life and the truth mirrored in the comic glass is made up of common custom—common not in the sense of a sociological or historical accident or even a statistical computation, but in the conceptual sense of a permanent and objective value in human affairs, common to all societies. "When I name Custome," Jonson observed, "I understand not the vulgar Custome: For that were a precept no lesse dangerous to Language, then life, if wee should speake or live after the manners of the vulgar: But that I call Custome of speech, which is the consent of the Learned; as Custom of life, which is the consent of the good" (*H & S*, 8: 622). The common customs make manifest what is normal and natural to human society, what is fitting and proper to life within it, what suits civilized living: in other words, the decorum of society, which in the seventeenth century could be called civility.

Indeed, so pervasive is Jonson's emphasis on propriety, measure, and order in *Discoveries* and so harsh is his exposure of the improper, the extravagant, and the disorderly in his plays that he may seem, to our eyes, uncommonly rigid in his strictures. Actually, in his own age and especially in the aristocratic and learned circles he moved in, his sense of social propriety and literary decorum was normal enough.[5] To Jonson, as to his age, Ulysses's famous speech on degree in *Troilus and Cressida* would have expressed not only a rationale for a world order and for a hierarchical society in it, but also the central norms in its theory of decorum:

---

5. A full discussion of the Renaissance conception of decorum appears in Bernard Weinberg, *A History of Literary Criticism in the Italian Renaissance* (Chicago, 1964), esp. pp. 71–72, 109, 182, 204, 436–37, 476, 485, 563, 746, 762, 801. In *Renaissance Literary Criticism* (Gloucester, Mass., 1959), Vernon Hall claims that decorum is essentially a "class concept" in the Renaissance in that it reflects the social distinctions of a hierarchical society (pp. 57–58, 210–11).

> The heavens themselves, the planets and this center
> Observe degree, propriety, and place,
> Insisture, course, proportion, season, form,
> Office, and custom, in all line of order . . .
>
> I.3.85–88

In fact, Jonson used several of these terms—propriety, proportion, and custom—in discussing decorum.

Again, he was quite conventional in his awareness of how many components must be considered in any question of decorum: age, sex, nature, character, nationality, profession, rank, financial condition. "In the difference of wits," he observed, "there are many notes," and mastery comes when one knows how "to discerne, what every nature, every disposition will beare . . . There are no fewer formes of minds, [than] of bodies amongst us" (*H & S*, 8: 584). Indeed, so numerous are these variables of body, mind, social status, and individual experience that "decorum" must be understood not as a single norm, but as a complex of norms. To perceive its operation in a comedy like *Epicoene*, then, requires that "ripenesse of Judgment," as Jonson put it, or that "learned and experienced discretion," as Puttenham put it, which only experience in the world and knowledge of past cultures can give.[6] Note, for one example, how Morose's reception of his bride-to-be expresses his eccentricity: "her temper of beauty has the true height of my blood" (II.5.17); that is, she is so beautiful that he desires her passionately; but in this indirect, preposterously abstract idiom passion is a remote and unlikely possibility. A few lines later, urging her to speak, he observes that the only sound he can endure is "the sweet voice of a fair lady" which, he says, "has the just length of my

---

6. See *H & S*, 8: 587 and 633, and George Puttenham, *The Arte of English Poesie*, ed. G. Willcock and A. Walker (London, 1936), p. 263. M. C. Bradbrook discusses decorum of dramatic speech and character sensibly in chapter 4 of *The Growth and Structure of Elizabethan Comedy* (1955).

ears." In such an asinine phrase he indeed speaks that we may see him.

The concept of the natural or decorum is in fact nowhere so active in the comedy of Jonson as when it is being violated in the characters' choice of words and their patterns of speech. As he noted in *Discoveries*, Jonson thought that in art as in life speech is "the Instrument of *Society*" (*H & S*, 8: 621). And in *Epicoene* each character is distinguished by speech which embodies his personal view of the world and reveals him as nothing else does. The Ladies Collegiate betray their pretentiousness, their lack of good taste, their failure to observe decorum, not merely by their foolish actions, but also by their foolish speech—which is, in dramatic fact, an especially revealing mode of action. When they speak, character and personality are embodied in their diction and syntax. Haughty's effusiveness and lack of discrimination are linguistically alive in the redundancy of her language. Haughty and Daw and all of the others are in their separate ways comic because they are measured against social and ethical standards which the play, usually by ironic implication, suggests. If one wants a more explicit statement of the standards which Jonson thought necessary to human cultures, one can turn to *Discoveries* where, with his usual deliberateness, he set down his own sense of stylistic and ethical norms. Of course, one must be careful not to assume automatically that the standards he prescribes as desirable in his criticism are the standards he uses as formative principles in his plays. The plays themselves, where these norms are implicit, must finally be appealed to.

Morose is clearly distinguished from such misusers of language as La Foole and Daw; he is not ambiguous or grammatically unsound, as they often are, nor does he use words incorrectly because ignorant of their meaning. His speech is indecorous because it lacks the poise and conversational ease that is "natural" to a man of breeding; it is cranky and bookish, and manifestly comes from the mouth of a man who, because of his egotism, has not listened to cultivated speech for some time and has lost its tune. Part of his ridiculousness comes from his thinking that he is courtly when again and again his speech proves him of an age long dead or never alive. As Morose is, so are the others: given a special voice and thereby a special comic life. To hear or to read *Epicoene*, or any other Jonsonian comedy, is to be jarred, sometimes lightly, sometimes emphatically, by inflation of image and maladjustment of diction, by inappropriate rhetorical schemes and hollow rhythms, all marking the deviation from decorum which defines, as it informs, the comic life of the play.

To insure that the audience is aware of this linguistic indecorum Jonson often uses one character to call attention to the speech of another. Thus Truewit, speaking of Mrs. Otter, directs Dauphine and Clerimont to "Mark her language," and soon after Dauphine observes, "What an excellent choice phrase this lady expresses in!" (III.2.13–24). He is referring to the clumsily inflated vocabulary that usually marks the pretender to gentility (*e.g.* "obnoxious or difficil," "resolve" to mean "inform"). Her "excellent choice phrase" comes from the court, but it comes second hand, from the patrons of her china shop; her use of it is thus comically indecorous. When she does speak in her own voice, it is in railing at her husband while she beats him: "You notorious, stinkardly bearward, does my breath smell?" (IV.2.102–03). Truewit ironically observes that she is "the only authentical courtier, that is not naturally bred one, in the city;" courtiers are naturally bred only at court, citizens (not then considered "gentle") in the city. Too fatuous and too vain to understand what is meant, Mrs. Otter complacently mistakes Truewit's judicious condemnation for praise. Care for details like these helped to produce Bishop King's praise of Jonson—praise echoed throughout the seventeenth century but too rarely heard since then, as one who taught a "ruder *Age*, / To speake by *Grammer*" so that by studying his language Englishmen might learn "the *heighth*, and *strength*, and *plentie* of their *owne*" (*H & S*, 11: 441). Stuart poets

and critics like King often called Jonson "correct" and "the model of decorum" because they were aware of how just his diction and how subtle the play of his syntax were.

Indeed, Jonson's command of syntax may have been more on King's mind when he wrote of height, strength, and plenty than the lexical virtuosity we have thus far noticed. Though Coleridge spoke of how much he admired "the *minutiae* of [Jonson's] rhythm, metre, choice of words, forms of connection," only modern criticism has analyzed these syntactical connections at any length. The most perceptive analysis is easily that of Jonas Barish, whose study of the speech of Truewit and Morose is especially rewarding. Truewit's "verbal prankishness" comes, Barish shows, from his sudden interpolations and whimsical flourishes working against an apparent balance; his spontaneity, from a doubling of elements—words, phrases, clauses—which gives a sense of rhythmic fullness, along with an avoiding of exact congruence. Morose's speech, at first affected in its magniloquent diction and fussy antitheses, then ridiculously agitated in its distraction, stands for a life trapped within the confines of itself and, in its sterility, for a kind of death.[7] Barish's whole chapter deserves a careful reading by anyone who wants to know how precisely controlled the art of *Epicoene* is.

Speech is central to this play about society because to Jonson it is central to human life itself. Morose does not suffer from noise as such so much as noise someone else makes. He is himself one of the most talkative persons in a play of magpies. But he hates "discourse," loving too much the sound of his own voice and the sense of his own mind. Often he asks the right question about language, as he does when he doubts the conventional greetings of the canon lawyer and the divine—"I wonder how these common forms, as 'God save you' and 'You are welcome,' are come to be a habit in our lives, or 'I am glad to see you!' when I cannot see what the profit can be of

7. Barish, *Ben Jonson and the Language of Prose Comedy* (Cambridge, Mass., 1960), pp. 149–66.

these words, so long as it is no whit better with him whose affairs are sad and grievous, that he hears this salutation" (V.3.23–27). It is the right question: what *is* the profit of such common forms of speech? But he asks it for the wrong reason: he is not interested in more useful conventions, and he does not really want to stop talking himself. In his next speech he tells the lawyer and the divine to let their comforts arrive quickly—and takes about two hundred words to say it.

So natural is speech to the human being that when a character in *Epicoene* enters a scene in which someone is silent he thinks something is wrong; thus Dauphine in I.2 wonders if Truewit and Clerimont are ill, they are so quiet, and in II.2 Truewit finds Morose and Mute as strange as fish because they are speechless. Speech seems to be associated with health and normal social activity—except by the egotistic Morose. Barish puts the point more strongly when he says that even as silence stands for impotence and death, "noise becomes the emblem of life, the inescapable ingredient of which normal existence is composed."[8] Mere talking, of course, is no sign of wisdom or even of sense. As Jonson reminds us, "For too much talking is ever the *Indice* of a foole" (*H & S*, 8: 574). He would have agreed with that collector of Elizabethan commonplaces, Robert Cawdrey, who wrote that "As emptie vessells make the loudest sound: So men of least wit, are the greatest bablers."[9] As always, Jonson asks us to see the complexity of things. Speech is human, but mere babbling can be done by idiots. Like all people who love language, he was aware of its limitations and made fun of those who take words too seriously. "What's six kicks to a man that reads Seneca?" (IV.5.260) says Truewit to the idiot Daw, as though reading a Stoic philosopher could keep pain from being painful!

Since language most reveals a man, Jonson uses it as a principal

8. Ibid., p. 183.

9. Cawdrey, *A Treasurie or Store-house of Similes* . . . (London, 1609), p. 854.

mode of social and moral discrimination. Speaking of Daw and La Foole, Barish notes that "Jonson shows first their verbal inadequacies, their pretentiousness of speech, and then develops the more specifically moral indictments of slander and cowardice." [10] Customarily Jonson uses speech to discriminate between the cultured and the pretenders to culture, the wits and the witless, the gentlemen and the boors, on the basis of the principle set down in the *Discoveries*: "To speake, and to speake well, are two things. A fool may talke, but a wise man speakes, and out of observation, knowledge, and use of things" (*H & S*, 8: 620). The gentleman, as Truewit reminds us, loves measure and judgment in all things because they are "gentlenesses"—that is, natural results of gentle breeding. But fools speak without measure and listen without thought. Even before Daw and La Foole are worked up to their heroic quarrel and their unheroic capitulation, Dauphine quiets Clerimont's fears that they may see through the plot: "Tut, flatter 'em both, as Truewit says, and you may take their understanding in a purse-net. They'll believe themselves to be just such men as we make, neither more nor less. They have nothing, not the use of their sense, but by tradition" (III.3.84–87). Daw and La Foole show the debasement of the power of words because they live only in the worst kind of tradition—hearsay, idle breath, empty fame.

Again, after the cowardice of the knights has been publicly demonstrated, and the ladies begin their court of Dauphine, Truewit points out how the Collegiates are "governed by crude opinion, without reason or cause." To Jonson "*Opinion* is a light, vaine, crude, and imperfect thing, settled in the Imagination; but never arriving at the understanding, there to obtaine the tincture of *Reason*" (*H & S*, 8: 564). His distinctions here echo the neo-Stoicism of Lipsius, who wrote in 1584 that the contrary of "right reason" (which he defined as the "true sense and judgment of things humane and divine") is opinion—"a false and frivolous conjecture

10. Barish, p. 169.

of those things."[11] In one of Jonson's masques, *Hymenaei*, the figures of Truth and Opinion appear together dressed so much alike that only the perceptive can distinguish one from the other. In *The Masque of Queens*, written about the time of *Epicoene*, there is an antimasque of hags and sorceresses representing Ignorance, False-hood, Credulity, Malice, Slander, Fury—all "opposites of glory" (*H & S*, 7: 318) and all represented less allegorically in *Epicoene*. Both the debased knights and the debasing ladies are cousins of those other worshipers of opinion, Erasmus's fools and Pope's dunces who know only what they are told, remember only what they were last told, and value only what is fashionable. "As they are informed," so they "believe, judge, praise, condemn, love, hate."

The pressure of the play's action opens these verbal discriminations out into larger moral and social judgments. What is normal for men and women? Who is the true gentleman? What is the proper marriage? What is the proper relationship between the natural and the artificial, or between the real and the apparent? What, finally, is the real? Since *Epicoene* is an ironic comedy, not a sermon or a case study, it does not categorically answer these questions but creates an image of life in which different possible points of view are comically represented and judged. Scene after scene pictures for us the various characters who deviate from the proper, customary ways of living. Thus we see men who are not as courageous as men are expected to be, and women who are not as modest as men think most women should be. We see a Sir Amorous more concerned with his clothes than a gentleman should be and are reminded that "Too much pickedness [elegance] is not manly" (*H & S*, 8: 607). We see the Collegiate Ladies, masculine in their authoritativeness, taming their husbands, setting up house on their own, pursuing lovers, and even incorporating themselves into a society. We see in the Otters a comic inversion of what the Jacobean age would have considered a normal

---

11. Justus Lipsius, *Two Bookes of Constancie* . . . Englished by Sir John Stradling, ed. R. Kirk (New Brunswick, N. J., 1939), pp. 79–80.

marriage. She reigns; he obeys. She allows him half a crown a day and a servant's maintenance. He objects to her only when he thinks she cannot know it, and is beaten by her when she does.

Jonson is not, of course, the only dramatist to create a malicious society of epicene creatures. As long ago as *Thesmophoriazusae*, as recently as *La Dolce Vita*, the drama has recurrently represented, usually comically, women who are aggressive or immodest in a way they are not supposed to be, and men who lack authority or courage or normal sexual interest in women. Perhaps, as Castiglione suggests, every man reaches a certain time in his life when he compares the present with the past and finds that in modern courts "there reigneth nothynge elles but envye and malyce, yll maners, and a most wanton lyfe in every kinde of vice: the women enticefull past shame, and the men womanishe."[12] Pamphleteers of the late sixteenth and early seventeenth centuries often found the loss of masculinity by men and of femininity by women an especially congenial subject for ridicule and castigation. From the flaming Phillip Stubbes, who anatomized the abuses of the 1580s, to the mystical Thomas Adams, who found the world a bedlam in the 1620s, English moralists used sexual deviation to represent the aberration of the age from the ways of God and nature. Three pamphlets of 1620 particularly express this theme—*Hic Mulier, the Man-Woman; Haec-Vir, or the Womanish-Man;* and *Muld Sacke, or the Apologie of Hic Mulier.* Of these, *Haec-Vir* may be the most relevant to the norms on which *Epicoene* depends. This pamphlet consists of a dialogue between Haec-Vir, the Womanish-Man, and Hic Mulier, the Man-Woman. Each accuses the other of unnaturalness, the mannish woman wanting to know why men curl their hair and rob women of their ruffs, fans and feathers, and even their sports and speech, the womanish man castigating women for their shorn locks and French doublets, their boots and spurs, and pistols.

12. Castiglione, *The Book of the Courtier*, trans. Sir Thomas Hoby (London, 1900), p. 106.

Hic Mulier claims that women, robbed of some of their essentially feminine characteristics by men, have taken, to their shame, those manly things forsaken by men. Especially have men forsaken horsemanship and the chivalric life so that arms rust, swords remain glued in scabbards, and nature has grown soft and effeminate.[13] *Epicoene* contains, at least implicitly, all that such pamphlets contain, but it presents us not so much a problem solved or a judgment made as an action simultaneously imitated, judged, and enjoyed.

Jonson does not directly involve, as the author of *Haec-Vir* does —in fact, as most pamphleteers do—"the Lawes of Nature, the rules of Religion," and "the Customes of all ciuill Nations" to justify a claim that there must be a distinct and special difference between men and women. He supposes that the audience of *Epicoene* has experience enough to know and judgment enough to apply such laws and customs to the images he offers them. Like all ironists, he works obliquely, peopling his plays with the prodigies, deviants, and dunces whose indirection can teach us how to find direction out. Thus Truewit, Clerimont, and Dauphine seem most truly witty and elegant gentlemen at first glance, and Jonson apparently asks us to share their aristocratic love of fools—a love that appears not merely in Truewit's obvious enjoyment of all the opportunities which Morose's ridiculous disease gives him of curing it, but also in such casual remarks as Dauphine's after Clerimont has described Sir Amorous La Foole: "Excellent! He was a fine youth last night, but now he is much finer!" (I.3.40–41). Minus its irony, what Dauphine is saying amounts to this: Sir Amorous was, I thought, a consummate idiot when I saw him last

13. *Haec-Vir* (London, 1620), Sig. C₁ verso and C₃ recto. Modern studies of these rare pamphlets appear in Louis Wright, *Middle-Class Culture in Elizabethan England* (Chapel Hill, 1935), pp. 465–507 and Chilton L. Powell, *English Domestic Relations, 1487–1653* (New York, 1917), pp. 166–69. I deal with this aspect of the play at greater length in *The Broken Compass: a Study of the Major Comedies of Ben Jonson* (New York, 1958), pp. 161–77.

night, but he has proved me wrong—he is so much more foolish today that I look to much greater pleasure from him in the future. To Dauphine and Truewit, as to the Dorimants and Valentines of a later age, fools possess one sovereign reason for being: they live to bring out the verbal wit of their betters. The fine gentlemen are not just playing with the fools, though they are certainly playing. They are also judging. Truewit thinks that his plot against Daw and La Foole is a legal process in which a charge is drawn up against these presumptuous fools and delivered by a sheriff (himself), and which involves a trial with judges (Dauphine, Clerimont, and himself) who shall render a verdict and mete out the proper punishment.

But while they are judging the fools, we are judging the judges. That Jonson sees their plots against Daw, La Foole, and Morose as at least partly judicial does not mean that he places himself on their side. Irony edges even the most admirable of his heroes and all but obliterates the least admirable. Nowhere does he require us to approve of his heroes uncritically—Volpone and Mosca, for example, or Dauphine and Truewit—however much we may enjoy the *élan* with which they carry out their deceptions or baitings. Indeed, the irony with which he treats them forbids our wholly approving them. Note how the vocatives "knights" and "gentlemen" bring an ironic perspective to the final act of *Epicoene*. Clerimont addresses Daw and La Foole as "knights" as he forces them to confess to a particularly unchivalrous act—their boast of having enjoyed the favors of Epicoene. Morose, overjoyed at what he thinks is his release, is worshipful to these "gentlemen," grateful to such "knights" (V.4.98–108). The fools are obviously not gentle or chivalric here; but neither are they wise. That Daw's question to Clerimont—"Is this gentlemanlike, sir?" (l. 83)—is not easy to answer unequivocally should suggest how complicated our moral response to the play must be. Daw and La Foole are clearly caricatures of true knights, but the authentic gentlemen are not always gentle, however genuinely manly they are.

The play's ironic exposure extends to the young gentlemen as well as the old, and we are called on to judge the perpetrators of torment, however gay they are, as well as the tormented, however afflicted they may be. Certainly when Morose, trusting himself to the good offices of Dauphine and Truewit, says, "I believe in you, and that deserves no delusion" (IV.7.32–3), we are to find the young gentlemen as comic in their duplicity as the old gentleman is in his blind trust. And when Dauphine dismisses Morose with "I'll not trouble you till you trouble me with your funeral, which I care not how soon it come," Jonson asks us to judge the propriety of that action as carefully as the propriety of Morose's earlier attempts to disinherit Dauphine. One legalistic judgment is that of Gifford (and Truewit): Morose's "ungenerous triumph over the imaginary distresses of his nephew . . . fully warrants the plot meditated against him in return." [14] We who watch all from outside can agree that, generally, in Jonson's plays, a malicious agent is rewarded with a malicious counter-action, but we are not called on to applaud one agent of malice while condemning another. We are expected to see and judge all. Dauphine's cool and heartless dismissal of his uncle places that young man with fine comic justice: he is one of Wilde's gentlemen who never hurt others—unintentionally.

The great achievement of *Epicoene* comes not simply from the discriminations which we must use our finest judgment to make, nor from the orchestration of its expressive voices which is so continuous a delight, nor even from its plot, so airily careless in movement and tightly coherent in structure. Its great achievement comes from the comic life which all of these—plot, character, ideas, and motifs—with much more, create and sustain, and from the joy which that life arouses in us richly and lastingly.

---

14. *The Works of Ben Jonson*, ed. W. Gifford (London, 1875), 3: 375–76, n. 7. But see Alfred Harbage, *Shakespeare and the Rival Traditions* (New York, 1952), p. 258.

To the Truly
Noble, by all
Titles,
Sir Francis Stuart

Sir,

My hope is not so nourished by example as it will conclude this dumb piece should please you, by cause it hath pleased others before, but by trust, that when you have read it, you will find it worthy to have displeased none. This makes that I now number you not only   5 in the names of favor but the names of justice to what I write; and do presently call you to the exercise of that noblest and manliest virtue, as coveting rather to be freed in my fame by the authority of a judge than the credit of an undertaker. Read therefore, I pray

---

3 by cause] because F₃.

SIR FRANCIS STUART *grandson of James Stewart, who was half brother of Mary, Queen of Scots, and appointed regent when she was forced to abdicate the throne in favor of her son. This dedication is evidently calculated to refute the charges of a 'libel' against the King's cousin, Lady Arabella Stuart, to which Jonson seems to refer in ll. 5. 11–16 below, and in* Another (*the second prologue*). *These charges are discussed in the Appendix. N. (N. refers throughout to a corresponding note at the end of the text.*)

1 AS *that.*

2 DUMB *silent (because printed, not performed).*

5 DISPLEASED NONE *N.*

  MAKES *causes (is the reason).*

9 CREDIT . . . UNDERTAKER *influence of a patron; backer; frequently, in political sense, "fixer"; cf. "names of favor," above, l. 6.*

you, and censure. There is not a line or syllable in it changed from 10
the simplicity of the first copy. And, when you shall consider, through
the certain hatred of some, how much a man's innocency may be
endangered by an uncertain accusation, you will, I doubt not, so
begin to hate the iniquity of such natures as I shall love the con-
tumely done me, whose end was so honorable as to be wiped off by 15
your sentence.

Your unprofitable but true lover,

Ben Jonson

10 CENSURE *judge*.

PROLOGUE

Truth says, of old the art of making plays
   Was to content the people, and their praise
   Was to the poet money, wine, and bays.
But in this age a sect of writers are
   That only for particular likings care   5
   And will taste nothing that is popular.
With such we mingle neither brains nor breasts.
   Our wishes, like to those make public feasts,
   Are not to please the cook's tastes, but the guests'.
Yet if those cunning palates hither come,   10
   They shall find guests' entreaty and good room;
   And though all relish not, sure there will be some
That, when they leave their seats, shall make 'em say,
   Who wrote that piece, could so have wrote a play,
   But that he knew this was the better way.   15
For to present all custard or all tart
   And have no other meats to bear a part,
   Or to want bread and salt, were but coarse art.
The poet prays you, then, with better thought

2 TO CONTENT THE PEOPLE *N.*
3 BAYS *leaves or sprigs of bay laurel, woven into a wreath or garland to honor a hero or poet.*
4 SECT OF WRITERS *N.*
8 THOSE MAKE *those who make.*
9 COOK'S TASTES *N.*
14 SO *according to the "particular likings" of l. 5 and the "cunning palates" of l.10.*

To sit, and when his cates are all in brought,   20
    Though there be none far-fet, there will dear-bought
Be fit for ladies; some for lords, knights, squires,
    Some for your waiting wench and city-wires,
    Some for your men and daughters of Whitefriars.
Nor is it only while you keep your seat   25
    Here that his feast will last, but you shall eat
    A week at ord'naries on his broken meat,
        If his muse be true,
        Who commends her to you.

20 CATES *provisions, choice and usually bought.*
21 FAR-FET *farfetched. Proverbial:* "*dere bought and far-fet / Are deinties for Ladies*" (*John Heywood,* Works, *I.xi*).
22–24 BE FIT FOR LADIES . . . WHITEFRIARS *N.*
23 CITY-WIRES *wires were used to support the ruff worn by Elizabethans; hence, a metonymy for a fashionable woman of the city.*
24 WHITEFRIARS *a* "*liberty*" *within the city of London, a refuge for lawbreakers. N.*
27 ORD'NARIES *taverns or eating houses.*

ANOTHER

The ends of all who for the Scene do write   *Occasioned by*
    Are, or should be, to profit and delight.   *some person's*
And still 't hath been the praise of all best times,   *impertinent*
    So persons were not touched, to tax the crimes.   *exception.*
Then, in this play which we present tonight,   5
    And make the object of your ear and sight,
On forfeit of yourselves, think nothing true,

SD *see Dedication: gloss to* "*Sir Francis Stuart*" *and N. to l. 5.*
1 SCENE *stage* (*Latin scena*).

24

Lest so you make the maker to judge you.
For he knows, poet never credit gained
    By writing truths, but things like truths well feigned.   10
If any yet will, with particular sleight
    Of application, wrest what he doth write,
And that he meant or him, or her, will say,
    They make a libel which he made a play.

11 PARTICULAR *special; here in the sense of personal, private.*
   SLEIGHT *crafty device or policy.*
12 WREST *twist, distort.*
13 AND . . . SAY *and will say that the poet has drawn one or another character from real life.*

The Persons of the Play

Morose, a gentleman that loves no noise
Dauphine Eugenie, a knight, his nephew
Clerimont, a gentleman, his friend
Truewit, another friend
Epicoene, a young gentleman supposed the silent woman
John Daw, a knight, her servant
Amorous La Foole, a knight also
Thomas Otter, a land and sea captain
Cutbeard, a barber
Mute, one of Morose's servants
Madam Haughty ⎫
Madam Centaure ⎬ Ladies Collegiates
Mrs. Mavis ⎭
Mrs. Trusty, the Lady Haughty's woman ⎫
Mrs. Otter, the Captain's wife ⎬ Pretenders
Parson
Pages
Servants

The Scene
LONDON

3 HIS *Dauphine's.*
6 SERVANT *lover devoted to the services of his mistress.*
10 MUTE *see N. to II.1.1. for the initial stage direction.*
11–13 LADIES COLLEGIATES *members of a fashionable clique, like a salon, with pretensions to the rights and privileges of a formal collegiate order. See I.1.69–80.*
14–15 PRETENDERS *aspirants to membership in the College.*

27

Act I Scene 1

[Clerimont's house.]

Clerimont. Ha' you got the song yet perfect I ga' you, boy?

[Clerimont] comes out making himself ready [followed by Boy.]

Boy. Yes, sir.

Clerimont. Let me hear it.

Boy. You shall, sir, but i'faith let nobody else.   5

Clerimont. Why, I pray?

Boy. It will get you the dangerous name of a poet in town, sir, besides me a perfect deal of ill will at the mansion you wot of, whose lady is the argument of it, where now I am the welcom'st thing under a man that comes there.   10

Clerimont. I think, and above a man too, if the truth were racked out of you.

Boy. No, faith, I'll confess before, sir. The gentlewomen play with me and throw me o' the bed, and carry me in to my lady, and she kisses me with her oiled face, and puts a peruke o' my head, and asks   15 me an' I will wear her gown, and I say no; and then she hits me a blow o' the ear and calls me innocent, and lets me go.

2–3 SD MAKING . . . READY *dressing.*

  8 WOT *know.*

15 PERUKE *wig worn as a fashionable headdress or as a cover for baldness (see l. 106).*

16 AN' *if ("and" in this sense will appear as "an'" throughout this edition).*

17 INNOCENT *simpleton.*

29

Clerimont. No marvel if the door be kept shut against your master, when the entrance is so easy to you. Well, sir, you shall go
20 there no more, lest I be fain to seek your voice in my lady's rushes a fortnight hence. Sing, sir. *Boy sings.*

[*Enter Truewit.*]

Truewit. Why, here's the man that can melt away his time, and never feels it! What between his mistress abroad and his ingle at home, high fare, soft lodging, fine clothes, and his fiddle, he thinks
25 the hours ha' no wings or the day no post-horse. Well, sir gallant, were you struck with the plague this minute or condemned to any capital punishment tomorrow, you would begin then to think and value every article o' your time, esteem it at the true rate and give all for't.

30 *Clerimont.* Why, what should a man do?

Truewit. Why, nothing, or that which, when 'tis done, is as idle. Harken after the next horse-race, or hunting-match; lay wagers, praise Puppy, or Pepper-corn, Whitefoot, Franklin; *Horses o' the* swear upon White-mane's party; spend aloud that my *time.*
35 lords may hear you; visit my ladies at night and be able to give 'em the character of every bowler or bettor o' the green. These be the things wherein your fashionable men exercise themselves, and I for company.

Clerimont. Nay, if I have thy authority, I'll not leave yet. Come,
40 the other are considerations when we come to have gray heads and weak hams, moist eyes and shrunk members. We'll think on 'em then; then we'll pray and fast.

20 RUSHES *straight green leaves of the rush, commonly used for strewing on the floors of houses.* N.

23 INGLE *an intimate or a boy kept for homosexual purposes; here apparently the latter.*

28 ARTICLE O' YOUR TIME *moment.*

39 LEAVE *give up (life of fashion).*

40 OTHER *i.e., view of life, as in ll. 25–29.*

41 HAMS *thighs and buttocks collectively.*

Truewit. Ay, and destine only that time of age to goodness which our want of ability will not let us employ in evil?

Clerimont. Why, then 'tis time enough. 45

Truewit. Yes, as if a man should sleep all the term and think to effect his business the last day. O, Clerimont, this time, because it is an incorporeal thing and not subject to sense, we mock ourselves the fineliest out of it, with vanity and misery indeed, not seeking an end of wretchedness, but only changing the matter still. 50

Clerimont. Nay, thou'lt not leave now—

Truewit. See but our common disease! With what justice can we complain that great men will not look upon us nor be at leisure to give our affairs such dispatch as we expect, when we will never do it ourselves, nor hear nor regard ourselves. 55

Clerimont. Foh! Thou hast read Plutarch's *Morals* now, or some such tedious fellow, and it shows so vilely with thee, 'fore God, 'twill spoil thy wit utterly. Talk me of pins, and feathers, and ladies, and rushes, and such things; and leave this stoicity alone till thou mak'st sermons. 60

Truewit. Well, sir, if it will not take, I have learned to lose as little of my kindness as I can. I'll do good to no man against his will, certainly. When were you at the college?

Clerimont. What college?

Truewit. As if you knew not! 65

46 TERM *one of the four periods into which the legal year was divided—Hilary, Easter, Trinity, Michaelmas.*

47 TIME *N.*

49 FINELIEST *most skilfully. N.*

56 PLUTARCH'S MORALS *the moral essays (called* Moralia) *of Plutarch (A.D. 45–120); see II.3.41–42 and N.*

58 WIT *here, intellectual capacity.*

59 RUSHES *see N. to l. 20 above. Hence, trifles.*

61 TAKE *succeed, be effective.*

63 COLLEGE *loosely, any association or fellowship; but "probationer" (l. 74) emphasizes college as an institution or "foundation" (ll. 67–68).*

Clerimont. No, faith, I came but from court yesterday.

Truewit. Why, is it not arrived there yet, the news? A new foundation, sir, here i' the town, of ladies that call themselves the
Collegiates, an order between courtiers and country-madams, that
70 live from their husbands and give entertainment to all the Wits and
Braveries o' the time, as they call 'em, cry down or up what they
like or dislike in a brain or a fashion with most masculine or rather
hermaphroditical authority, and every day gain to their college
some new probationer.

75 *Clerimont.* Who is the president?

Truewit. The grave and youthful matron, the Lady Haughty.

Clerimont. A pox of her autumnal face, her pieced beauty! There's
no man can be admitted till she be ready nowadays, till she has
painted and perfumed and washed and scoured, but the boy here,
80 and him she wipes her oiled lips upon like a sponge. I have made a
song, I pray thee hear it, o' the subject.

SONG   [*Boy sings.*]

Still to be neat, still to be dressed,
As you were going to a feast;
Still to be powdered, still perfumed:
85 Lady, it is to be presumed,
Though art's hid causes are not found,
All is not sweet, all is not sound.

Give me a look, give me a face,
That makes simplicity a grace;

69–73 COLLEGIATES . . . AUTHORITY *N*.

70–71 WITS . . . BRAVERIES *i.e., as arbiters of fashionable talk and fashionable dress
respectively.*

77 A POX OF *a curse on*.
   PIECED *patched, mended*.

79–113 SCOURED . . . FINISHED *N*.

82–93 SONG *N*.

82 STILL *always*. NEAT *carefully elegant*.

Robes loosely flowing, hair as free: 90
Such sweet neglect more taketh me
Than all th'adulteries of art.
They strike mine eyes, but not my heart.

Truewit. And I am clearly o' the other side: I love a good dressing
before any beauty o' the world. O, a woman is then like a delicate   95
garden, nor is there one kind of it: she may vary every hour, take
often counsel of her glass and choose the best. If she have good ears,
show 'em; good hair, lay it out; good legs, wear short clothes; a
good hand, discover it often; practice any art to mend breath, cleanse
teeth, repair eyebrows, paint, and profess it.   100

Clerimont. How! Publicly?

Truewit. The doing of it, not the manner: that must be private.
Many things that seem foul i' the doing, do please, done. A lady
should indeed study her face, when we think she sleeps; nor when
the doors are shut should men be inquiring; all is sacred within, then.   105
Is it for us to see their perukes put on, their false teeth, their complexion, their eyebrows, their nails? You see gilders will not work
but enclosed. They must not discover how little serves with the
help of art to adorn a great deal. How long did the canvas hang
afore Aldgate? Were the people suffered to see the city's *Love* and   110
Charity while they were rude stone, before they were painted and
burnished? No. No more should servants approach their mistresses
but when they are complete and finished.

Clerimont. Well said, my Truewit.

Truewit. And a wise lady will keep a guard always upon the   115
place, that she may do things securely. I once followed a rude

91 TAKETH *captivates* (OED).
92 ADULTERIES *adulteration* (OED).
97 GLASS *mirror, looking-glass.*
107 GILDERS *those who covered base metals with a thin layer of gold* (OED).
108 DISCOVER *reveal.*
110–13 ALDGATE . . . FINISHED *N.*

33

fellow into a chamber, where the poor madam, for haste, and troubled, snatched at her peruke to cover her baldness and put it on the wrong way.

120   *Clerimont.* O prodigy!

Truewit. And the unconscionable knave held her in compliment an hour, with that reversed face, when I still looked when she should talk from the t'other side.

Clerimont. Why, thou shouldst ha' relieved her.

125   *Truewit.* No, faith, I let her alone, as we'll let this argument, if you please, and pass to another. When saw you Dauphine Eugenie?

Clerimont. Not these three days. Shall we go to him this morning? He is very melancholic, I hear.

Truewit. Sick o' the uncle, is he? I met that stiff piece of formality,
130   his uncle, yesterday, with a huge turbant of nightcaps on his head, buckled over his ears.

Clerimont. O, that's his custom when he walks abroad. He can endure no noise, man.

Truewit. So I have heard. But is the disease so ridiculous in him as
135   it is made? They say he has been upon divers treaties with the fish-wives and orange-women, and articles propounded between them. Marry, the chimney-sweepers will not be drawn in.

Clerimont. No, nor the broom-men: they stand out stiffly. He cannot endure a costermonger, he swoons if he hear one.

140   *Truewit.* Methinks a smith should be ominous.

---

120 PRODIGY *something abnormal or monstrous.*

121 COMPLIMENT *formal expressions of courtesy.*

129 SICK O' THE UNCLE " *Modelled on 'sick of the mother' (hysteria)*" (*H & S*).

130 TURBANT *turban.*

135–36 FISHWIVES *N.*

    ARTICLES *points of an agreement or treaty.*

138 STAND OUT *refuse to join* (*in the articles propounded between Morose and the noisy women*).

139 COSTERMONGER *a seller of apples who usually sold his fruit in the open street.*

Clerimont. Or any hammer-man. A brazier is not suffered to dwell in the parish, nor an armorer. He would have hanged a pewterer's 'prentice once upon a Shrove Tuesday's riot for being o' that trade, when the rest were quit.

Truewit. A trumpet should fright him terribly, or the hautboys? 145

Clerimont. Out of his senses. The waits of the city have a pension of him not to come near that ward. This youth practiced on him one night like the bellman, and never left till he had brought him down to the door with a long sword, and there left him flourishing with the air. 150

Boy. Why, sir, he hath chosen a street to lie in so narrow at both ends that it will receive no coaches nor carts nor any of these common noises, and therefore we that love him devise to bring him in such as we may, now and then, for his exercise, to breathe him. He would grow resty else in his ease. His virtue would rust with- 155 out action. I entreated a bearward one day to come down with the dogs of some four parishes that way, and I thank him he did, and cried his games under Master Morose's windore till he was sent crying away with his head made a most bleeding spectacle to the

141 HAMMER-MAN *any worker in metal: the two kinds noted—workers in brass and in pewter—might then have been especially noisy.*

143 SHROVE TUESDAY'S RIOT *apprentices usually celebrated this holiday by wrecking brothels.*

144 QUIT *acquitted.*

145 HAUTBOYS *oboes.*

146 WAITS *N.*

147 THIS YOUTH *the Boy.*

147–48 PRACTICED . . . BELLMAN *harassed Morose by performing outside his house like a bellman, or night watchman (OED), i.e., calling the hours and ringing a bell.*

154 BREATHE *exercise briskly; said of horses.*

155 RESTY *either restive (said of horses who stubbornly stand still) or sluggish.*

156 BEARWARD *the keeper of a bear, who led it about for public exhibitions.*

158 WINDORE *window.*

160 multitude. And, another time, a fencer, marching to his prize, had his drum most tragically run through, for taking that street in his way, at my request.

    Truewit. A good wag. How does he for the bells?

    Clerimont. O, i' the Queen's time he was wont to go out of town
165 every Saturday at ten o'clock or on holiday eves. But now, by reason of the sickness, the perpetuity of ringing has made him devise a room with double walls and treble ceilings, the windores close shut and calked, and there he lives by candlelight. He turned away a man last week for having a pair of new shoes that creaked,
170 and this fellow waits on him now in tennis-court socks, or slippers soled with wool, and they talk each to other in a trunk. See who comes here

165 holiday] holy day F.

––––––––

160 PRIZE *fencing-match (as in "prizefight"); professional fencers could be drummed through the city to increase interest in their matches.*

163–66 BELLS . . . SICKNESS *N.*

165 HOLIDAY *the differences in form and meaning were not as marked as they have become.*

171 TRUNK *speaking tube.*

Act I Scene 2

[*Enter Dauphine.*]

    Dauphine. How now! What ail you, sirs? Dumb?

    Truewit. Struck into stone almost, I am here, with tales o' thine uncle! There was never such a prodigy heard of.

    Dauphine. I would you would once lose this subject, my masters,

4 ONCE *once for all.*

for my sake. They are such as you are, that have brought me into that   5
predicament I am with him.

Truewit. How is that?

Dauphine. Marry, that he will disinherit me, no more. He thinks
I and my company are authors of all the ridiculous acts and monuments are told of him.   10

Truewit. 'Slid, I would be the author of more to vex him; that
purpose deserves it: it gives thee law of plaguing him. I'll tell thee
what I would do. I would make a false almanac, get it printed, and
then ha' him drawn out on a coronation day to the Tower-wharf,
and kill him with the noise of the ordnance. Disinherit thee! He   15
cannot, man. Art not thou next of blood, and his sister's son?

Dauphine. Ay, but he will thrust me out of it, he vows, and marry.

Truewit. How! That's a more portent. Can he endure no noise,
and will venture on a wife?

Clerimont. Yes. Why, thou art a stranger, it seems, to his best trick   20
yet. He has employed a fellow this half year all over England to
harken him out a dumb woman, be she of any form or any quality,
so she be able to bear children. Her silence is dowry enough, he says.

Truewit. But I trust to God he has found none.

Clerimont. No, but he has heard of one that's lodged i' the next   25

---

9 ACTS ... MONUMENTS *reference to Morose's martyrdom and Foxe's* Book of
   Martyrs *whose first English edition (1563) had as its title* Actes and Monuments.
11 'SLID *abbrev. of "God's lid" (eyelid); an oath common in the seventeenth
   century.*
11–12 THAT PURPOSE *i.e., Morose's disinheriting Dauphine.*
   GIVES THEE LAW *authorizes you.*
14 CORONATION DAY *the guns of the Tower saluted the King on his birthday and on
   the anniversary of his coronation.*
18 A MORE PORTENT *a greater portent: marriage might produce children, whereas
   disinheriting seems illegal (see ll. 15–16).*
22 HARKEN *find by inquiry.*
   QUALITY *rank.*

street to him, who is exceedingly soft-spoken, thrifty of her speech, that spends but six words a day. And her he's about now and shall have her.

    Truewit. Is't possible! Who is his agent i' the business?

30   *Clerimont*. Marry, a barber, one Cutbeard, an honest fellow, one that tells Dauphine all here.

    Truewit. Why, you oppress me with wonder! A woman and a barber, and love no noise!

    Clerimont. Yes, faith. The fellow trims him silently and has not
35 the knack with his shears or his fingers, and that continence in a barber he thinks so eminent a virtue as it has made him chief of his counsel.

    Truewit. Is the barber to be seen? Or the wench?

    Clerimont. Yes, that they are.

40   *Truewit*. I pray thee, Dauphine, let's go thither.

    Dauphine. I have some business now; I cannot i' faith.

    Truewit. You shall have no business shall make you neglect this, sir. We'll make her talk, believe it; or if she will not, we can give out at least so much as shall interrupt the treaty; we will break it.
45 Thou art bound in conscience, when he suspects thee without cause, to torment him.

    Dauphine. Not I, by any means. I'll give no suffrage to't. He shall never ha' that plea against me that I opposed the least fant'sy of his. Let it lie upon my stars to be guilty, I'll be innocent.

50   *Truewit*. Yes, and be poor, and beg; do, innocent, when some

32–33 WOMAN . . . BARBER *N*.

35 KNACK *sharp crack or snap.*

45 IN CONSCIENCE *by all that is right. N.*

47 SUFFRAGE *consent.*

48 FANT'SY *fancy; and so pronounced, but full contraction obscures the range of meaning available—e.g., caprice, amorous passion, delusion.*

49 LET . . . STARS *though I be fated.*

groom of his has got him an heir, or this barber, if he himself cannot. Innocent! I pray thee, Ned, where lies she? Let him be innocent still.

Clerimont. Why, right over against the barber's, in the house where Sir John Daw lies. 55

Truewit. You do not mean to confound me!

Clerimont. Why?

Truewit. Does he that would marry her know so much?

Clerimont. I cannot tell.

Truewit. 'Twere enough of imputation to her, with him. 60

Clerimont. Why?

Truewit. The only talking sir i' th' town! Jack Daw! And he teach her not to speak—God be w' you. I have some business too.

Clerimont. Will you go thither then?

Truewit. Not with the danger to meet Daw, for mine ears. 65

Clerimont. Why? I thought you two had been upon very good terms.

Truewit. Yes, of keeping distance.

Clerimont. They say he is a very good scholar.

Truewit. Ay, and he says it first. A pox on him, a fellow that 70 pretends only to learning, buys titles, and nothing else of books in him.

Clerimont. The world reports him to be very learned.

Truewit. I am sorry the world should so conspire to belie him.

Clerimont. Good faith, I have heard very good things come from 75 him.

---

54 OVER AGAINST *opposite to.*

56 CONFOUND ME *confuse or astound me.*

60 IMPUTATION *accusation: i.e., the reticence of any woman would be made suspect simply by her living with the talkative Daw.*

62 ONLY *peerless.*

71 TITLES *of books; not his knighthood.*

Truewit. You may. There's none so desperately ignorant to deny that; would they were his own. God be w' you, gentlemen. [*Exit.*]

Clerimont. This is very abrupt!

78 God be w'you] God b'w'you F.

---

78 GOD . . . YOU *good-bye; to represent the contraction precisely in print is awkward as well as difficult. In the iambic pentameter of his verse plays, Jonson can treat it as a single foot (e.g.,* The Alchemist, *I.1.197*).

Act I Scene 3

Dauphine. Come, you are a strange open man to tell everything thus.

Clerimont. Why, believe it, Dauphine, Truewit's a very honest fellow.

5 *Dauphine.* I think no other, but this frank nature of his is not for secrets.

Clerimont. Nay, then, you are mistaken, Dauphine. I know where he has been well trusted, and discharged the trust very truly and heartily.

10 *Dauphine.* I contend not, Ned, but, with the fewer a business is carried, it is ever the safer. Now we are alone, if you'll go thither, I am for you.

Clerimont. When were you there?

Dauphine. Last night, and such a *Decameron* of sport fallen out! 15 Boccace never thought of the like. Daw does nothing but court her,

1 STRANGE OPEN *surprisingly outspoken (taking "strange" as an adv. formed from an adj.).*

11 THITHER *to visit Epicoene.*

14–15 DECAMERON . . . BOCCACE *Boccaccio's collection of one hundred tales, many about foolish lovers and duped husbands.*

FALLEN OUT *happened, came to pass.*

and the wrong way. He would lie with her, and praises her modesty;
desires that she would talk and be free, and commends her silence in
verses, which he reads and swears are the best that ever man made.
Then rails at his fortunes, stamps, and mutines why he is not made a
counsellor and called to affairs of state.   20

Clerimont. I pray thee, let's go. I would fain partake this. Some
water, Boy. [*Exit Boy.*]

Dauphine. We are invited to dinner together, he and I, by one
that came thither to him, Sir La Foole.

Clerimont. O' that's a precious manikin!   25

Dauphine. Do you know him?

Clerimont. Ay, and he will know you too, if e'er he saw you but
once, though you should meet him at church in the midst of
prayers. He is one of the Braveries, though he be none o' the Wits.
He will salute a judge upon the bench and a bishop in the pulpit, a   30
lawyer when he is pleading at the bar, and a lady when she is dancing in a masque, and put her out. He does give plays and suppers,
and invites his guests to 'em aloud, out of his windore as they ride
by in coaches. He has a lodging in the Strand for the purpose. Or to
watch when ladies are gone to the china-houses or the Exchange, that 35
he may meet 'em by chance, and give 'em presents, some two or
three hundred pounds' worth of toys, to be laughed at. He is never

19 MUTINES WHY *rebels because.*

21 FAIN PARTAKE *adv.* + *trans. verb:* "*gladly take part in.*"

25 MANIKIN *little man: i.e., not very manly, or a diminutive imitation, like a
puppet.*

32 PUT HER OUT *disconcert or upset her so that she forgets her part in the dance.*

34 STRAND *a street once occupying the "strand" or shore of the Thames between
London and Westminster; early in the seventeenth century a place where many of
the gentry lived.*

35 CHINA-HOUSES *shops where exotic and expensive products from the Orient were
displayed; frequently mentioned as fashionable meeting-places.*
EXCHANGE *the New Exchange in the Strand, a market built in 1608–09,
especially noted for its fashionable ladies' shops.*

37 TOYS *trinkets; rubbish.*

without a spare banquet or sweetmeats in his chamber, for there women to alight at and come up to for a bait.

40   *Dauphine.* Excellent! He was a fine youth last night, but now he is much finer! What is his Christian name? I ha' forgot.

[Re-enter Boy.]

    Clerimont. Sir Amorous La Foole.

    Boy. The gentleman is here below that owns that name.

    Clerimont. 'Heart, he's come to invite me to dinner, I hold my life.

45   *Dauphine.* Like enough. Pray thee, let's ha' him up.

    Clerimont. Boy, marshal him.

    Boy. With a truncheon, sir?

    Clerimont. Away, I beseech you. *[Exit Boy.]* I'll make him tell us his pedigree now, and what meat he has to dinner, and who are his

50 guests, and the whole course of his fortunes, with a breath.

38 there] their, before F. reset (Beaurline).

---

38 BANQUET *here, a course of sweetmeats, fruit, and wine.*

39 BAIT *a quibble; food as refreshment, and as a lure.*

44 'HEART *exclamation of surprise, as now in "Bless my heart."*
    HOLD *bet: "bet my life".*

46 MARSHAL *conduct ceremoniously.*

47 TRUNCHEON *pun on: 1. marshal's baton; 2. cudgel.*

50 BREATH *N.*

Act I Scene 4

[Enter La Foole.]

    La Foole. 'Save, dear Sir Dauphine, honored Master Clerimont.

    Clerimont. Sir Amorous! You have very much honested my lodging with your presence.

1 'SAVE *an affectedly lazy form of "God save you."*

2 HONESTED *honored.*

La Foole. Good faith, it is a fine lodging, almost as delicate a lodging as mine. 5

Clerimont. Not so, sir.

La Foole. Excuse me, sir, if it were i' the Strand, I assure you. I am come, Master Clerimont, to entreat you wait upon two or three ladies to dinner today.

Clerimont. How, sir! Wait upon 'em? Did you ever see me carry 10 dishes?

La Foole. No, sir, dispense with me; I meant, to bear 'em company.

Clerimont. O, that I will, sir. The doubtfulness o' your phrase, believe it, sir, would breed you a quarrel once an hour with the 15 terrible boys, if you should but keep 'em fellowship a day.

La Foole. It should be extremely against my will, sir, if I contested with any man.

Clerimont. I believe it, sir. Where hold you your feast?

La Foole. At Tom Otter's, sir. 20

Dauphine. Tom Otter? What's he?

La Foole. Captain Otter, sir; he is a kind of gamester, but he has had command both by sea and by land.

Dauphine. O, then he is *animal amphibium*?

---

4 GOOD FAITH *like "i'faith" or "faith"—interjections derived from the phrase "in good faith," in truth, really.*

10–12 WAIT UPON . . . DISPENSE *N.*

16 TERRIBLE BOYS *riotous youths of Jacobean London; also called "roaring boys"; somewhat like England's "teddy boys" and the older members of our juvenile gangs.*

22 GAMESTER *gambler; frolicsome person.*

24 ANIMAL AMPHIBIUM *a creature of two natures, partly because he has had amphibious command (l. 23), partly because, being subject to his masculine wife, he belongs to the "epicene gender"—somewhere between man and woman. See Persons of the Play and N.*

25   *La Foole.* Ay, sir. His wife was the rich china-woman that the courtiers visited so often, that gave the rare entertainment. She commands all at home.

    Clerimont. Then she is Captain Otter?

    La Foole. You say very well, sir. She is my kinswoman, a La Foole

30   by the mother side, and will invite any great ladies for my sake.

    Dauphine. Not of the La Fooles of Essex?

    La Foole. No, sir, the La Fooles of London.

    Clerimont. [*Aside.*] Now, he's in.

    La Foole. They all come out of our house, the La Fooles o' the

35   north, the La Fooles of the west, the La Fooles of the east and south—we are as ancient a family as any is in Europe—but I myself am descended lineally of the French La Fooles—and we do bear for our coat *yellow*, or *or*, checkered *azure* and *gules*, and some three or four colors more, which is a very noted coat and has sometimes

40   been solemnly worn by divers nobility of our house—but let that go, antiquity is not respected now—I had a brace of fat does sent me, gentlemen, and half a dozen of pheasants, a dozen or two of godwits, and some other fowl, which I would have eaten while they are good, and in good company—there will be a great lady or two,

45   my Lady Haughty, my Lady Centaure, Mistress Dol Mavis—and they come o' purpose to see the silent gentlewoman, Mistress Epicoene, that honest Sir John Daw has promised to bring thither—and

---

25 CHINA-WOMAN *a woman keeping a china-shop, but because china-houses were often said to be places of assignation, Sir Amorous ineptly manages to suggest that his kinswoman (l. 29) once ran something like a call house.*

30 MOTHER SIDE *mother's side: 's dropped for euphony, as in "riverside."*

33 IN *adv.: now he's taken the bait.*

38 COAT *of arms.* OR *gold used in armorial bearing.*
    GULES *the heraldic color, red. See IV.5.291.*

38–39 THREE . . . MORE *La Foole unwittingly suggests the fool's motley—i.e., the many-colored dress of the professional jester.*

43 GODWITS *marsh-birds, once a great delicacy.*

then Mistress Trusty, my Lady's woman, will be there too, and this honorable knight, Sir Dauphine, with yourself, Master Clerimont—and we'll be very merry and have fiddlers, and dance—I have been a 50 mad wag in my time, and have spent some crowns since I was a page in court to my Lord Lofty, and after, my Lady's gentleman-usher, who got me knighted in Ireland, since it pleased my elder brother to die—I had as fair a gold jerkin on that day as any was worn in the Island Voyage or at Cadiz, none dispraised, and I came over in it 55 hither, showed myself to my friends in court and after went down to my tenants in the country and surveyed my lands, let new leases, took their money, spent it in the eye o' the land here, upon ladies—and now I can take up at my pleasure.

   Dauphine. Can you take up ladies, sir? 60

   Clerimont. O, let him breath, he has not recovered.

   Dauphine. Would I were your half in that commodity—

   La Foole. No, sir, excuse me; I meant money, which can take up anything. I have another guest or two to invite and say as much to, gentlemen. I'll take my leave abruptly, in hope you will not fail— 65 Your servant. [*Exit La Foole.*]

---

55 Cadiz] Caliz F.

---

52 GENTLEMAN-USHER *a gentleman who attends to, or goes before a person of high rank.*

53 KNIGHTED *N.*

54 GOLD JERKIN *close-fitting jacket, often made of leather; one of gold would immediately stamp the wearer as a gallant.*

55 ISLAND VOYAGE *N.*

   CADIZ *Spanish port attacked by Essex and Lord Howard in 1596.*

57–59 TENANTS . . . PLEASURE *N.*

58 EYE *center or seat of light.*

59, 63 TAKE UP *1. receive (money from rents); 2. buy up or hire (ladies or "anything").*

61 BREATH *take a breath.*

62 COMMODITY *anything one trades in. Dauphine means "ladies."*

Act I Scene 4

Dauphine. We will not fail you, sir precious La Foole; but she shall that your ladies come to see, if I have credit afore Sir Daw.

Clerimont. Did you ever hear such a wind-fucker as this?

70 *Dauphine.* Or such a rook as the other, that will betray his mistress to be seen? Come, 'tis time we prevented it.

Clerimont. Go. [*Exeunt.*]

69 wind-fucker] wind-sucker, 1692 F. and later eds. See fn.

---

68 AFORE *in precedence of, above.*

69 WIND-FUCKER *the kestrel or windhover, so-called "from its habit of hovering or hanging in the air with its head to the wind."* (OED).

70 ROOK *crow; fig., simpleton, gull; see Persons of the Play and N.*
   OTHER *Daw.*

Act II Scene 1

[*Morose's house. Enter Morose with speaking-tube in his hand, followed by Mute.*]

Morose. Cannot I yet find out a more compendious method than by this trunk to save my servants the labor of speech and mine ears the discord of sounds? Let me see. All discourses but mine own afflict me; they seem harsh, impertinent, and irksome. Is it not possible that thou shouldst answer me by signs, and I apprehend thee, fellow? 5
Speak not, though I question you. You have taken the ring off from the street door, as I bade you? Answer me not by speech but by silence, unless it be otherwise—[*Mute makes a leg.*]—very good. *At the breaches, still the fellow makes legs, or signs.*
And you have fastened on a thick quilt or flock-bed on the outside of the door, that if they knock with their 10
daggers or with brickbats, they can make no noise? But with your leg, your answer, unless it be otherwise—[*Makes a leg.*]—very good. This is not only fit modesty in a servant, but good state and

1 SD MUTE *Morose's servant; "mute" was the technical name for an actor who performed in pantomime or dumb show. N.*

6 RING *knocker.*

8 SD BREACHES *breaks in the text, referring to dashes used in the F. text to mark the servant's responses, indicated in this edition by separate stage directions.*

9 SD MAKES LEGS *bows, specifically by bending one leg and drawing back the other; a customary form of deference.*

FLOCK-BED *quilt made of flock (tufts of wool or cotton).*

13 STATE *dignified observance of ceremony.*

discretion in a master. And you have been with Cutbeard, the barber,
to have him come to me? [*Makes a leg.*]—good. And he will come
presently? Answer me not but with your leg, unless it be otherwise;
if it be otherwise, shake your head or shrug—[*Makes a leg.*]—so.
Your Italian and Spaniard are wise in these, and it is a frugal and
comely gravity. How long will it be ere Cutbeard come? Stay; if
an hour, hold up your whole hand; if half an hour, two fingers; if a
quarter, one—[*Holds up one finger bent.*]—good; half a quarter? 'Tis
well. And have you given him a key to come in without knocking?
[*Makes a leg.*]—good. And is the lock oiled, and the hinges, today?
[*Makes a leg.*]—good. And the quilting of the stairs nowhere worn
out and bare? [*Makes a leg.*]—very good. I see by much doctrine and
impulsion, it may be effected. Stand by. The Turk, in this divine
discipline, is admirable, exceeding all the potentates of the earth;
still waited on by mutes, and all his commands so executed, yea,
even in the war, as I have heard, and in his marches, most of his charges
and directions given by signs and with silence: an exquisite art!
And I am heartily ashamed and angry oftentimes that the princes of
Christendom should suffer a barbarian to transcend 'em in so high
a point of felicity. I will practise it hereafter. How *One winds a horn without.*
now? Oh! oh! what villain, what prodigy of mankind
is that?

Look! [*Exit Mute.*] Oh! cut his throat, cut his throat! *[Horn] Again.*
What murderer, hell-hound, devil can this be?

[*Re-enter Mute.*]

Mute. It is a post from the court—

18–19 ITALIAN . . . GRAVITY *See the Turk, l. 26 below, and N.*

25 DOCTRINE *teaching.*

26 IMPULSION *instigation.*

26–33 TURK . . . FELICITY *N.*

34 SD WINDS *blows.*

PRODIGY *monster.*

38 POST *one who traveled express with letters or messages and who often announced his arrival by blowing a horn.*

Morose. Out, rogue! And must thou blow thy horn, too?

Mute. Alas, it is a post from the court, sir, that says he must speak   40
with you, pain of death—

Morose. Pain of thy life, be silent!

Act II Scene 2

[*Enter Truewit carrying a post-horn and a halter.*]

Truewit. By your leave, sir—I am a stranger here—is your name
Master Morose? [*Turns from Morose to Mute.*] Is your name Master
Morose? Fishes, Pythagoreans all! This is strange! What say you,
sir? Nothing? Has Harpocrates been here with his club among you?
Well, sir, I will believe you to be the man at this time; I will venture   5
upon you, sir. Your friends at court commend 'em to you, sir—

Morose. O men! O manners! Was there ever such an impudence?

Truewit. —And are extremely solicitous for you, sir.

Morose. Whose knave are you?

Truewit. Mine own knave and your compeer, sir.   10

Morose. Fetch me my sword—

Truewit. You shall taste the one half of my dagger, if you do,
groom, and you the other if you stir, sir. Be patient, I charge you,

---

3 FISHES *i.e.*, *dumb.*

  PYTHAGOREANS *said to have undergone novitiate of five years' silence; and as
  a sect, noted for secrecy.*

4 HARPOCRATES *N.*

5–6 VENTURE UPON *make trial of or dare to approach.*

7 O MEN! O MANNERS! *like Cicero's "O tempora, O mores," which Jonson
  translated as "O age, and manners" in* Cataline, *IV.190.*

10 COMPEER *an equal or associate.*

in the king's name, and hear me without insurrection. They say you
15   are to marry? To marry! Do you mark, sir?

    Morose. How then, rude companion!

    Truewit. Marry, your friends do wonder, sir, the Thames being
so near, wherein you may drown so handsomely; or London Bridge
at a low fall, with a fine leap, to hurry you down the stream; or such
20   a delicate steeple i' the town as Bow, to vault from; or a braver height
as Paul's; or if you affected to do it nearer home and a shorter way,
an excellent garret windore into the street; or a beam   *He shows him a*
in the said garret, with this halter, which they have   *halter.*
sent, and desire that you would sooner commit your grave head to
25   this knot than to the wedlock noose; or take a little sublimate and go
out of the world like a rat, or a fly, as one said, with a straw i' your
arse: any way rather than to follow this goblin Matrimony. Alas,
sir, do you ever think to find a chaste wife in these times? Now?
When there are so many masques, plays, Puritan preachings, mad
30   folks, and other strange sights to be seen daily, private and public?

---

17 Marry] Mary F.
22 windore] window F₂.

14–15 THEY . . . MARRY *N.*

17 MARRY *interj. (orig. in oaths, the Virgin Mary), an exclamation of surprise,*
indignation; perhaps a quibble: as if the verb "to marry" were itself an expression
of surprise, indignation, and "wonder."

19 LOW FALL *ebb tide.*

20 BOW *the "delicate steeple" of this Cheapside church can be seen in Visscher's*
View of London (*1616*).

21 PAUL'S *the roof of St. Paul's Church; the steeple, burned in 1561, was never*
replaced.

25 SUBLIMATE *"mercury sublimate" or mercuric chloride, which acts as a violent*
poison, was once used to kill rats.

26 FLY *William Harrison describes fly and spider fights staged by idle fellows who*
impaled a fly on a piece of straw, apparently to immobilize it (Description of
England, *ed. F. Furnivall [London, 1879], 2: 39 [III, chap. vi]*).

If you had lived in King Ethelred's time, sir, or Edward the Con-
fessor's, you might, perhaps, have found in some cold country
hamlet then, a dull frosty wench would have been contented with
one man; now, they will as soon be pleased with one leg or one eye.
I'll tell you, sir, the monstrous hazards you shall run with a wife.   35

Morose. Good sir, have I ever cozened any friends of yours of
their land? bought their possessions? taken forfeit of their mortgage?
begged a reversion from 'em? bastarded their issue? What have I
done that may deserve this?

Truewit. Nothing, sir, that I know, but your itch of marriage.   40

Morose. Why? If I had made an assassinate upon your father,
vitiated your mother, ravished your sisters—

Truewit. I would kill you, sir, I would kill you if you had.

Morose. Why? You do more in this, sir. It were a vengeance cen-
tuple for all facinorous acts that could be named, to do that you do.   45

Truewit. Alas, sir, I am but a messenger; I but tell you what you
must hear. It seems your friends are careful after your soul's health,
sir, and would have you know the danger—but you may do your
pleasure for all them; I persuade not, sir. If, after you are married,
your wife do run away with a vaulter, or the Frenchman that walks   50
upon ropes, or him that dances the jig, or a fencer for his skill at his
weapon, why, it is not their fault; they have discharged their con-
sciences when you know what may happen. Nay, suffer valiantly,
sir, for I must tell you all the perils that you are obnoxious to. If she

31 ETHELRED . . . EDWARD *Kings of England, 978–1016 and 1042–1066.*

33 WOULD *who would.*

37 TAKEN FORFEIT *taken up a mortgage because of a penalty for breach of contract;
roughly, foreclose.*

38 REVERSION *an estate returned to a grantor after the grant has expired.*

41 MADE AN ASSASSINATE *a fussy way to say "murder."*

42 VITIATED *violated.*

45 FACINOROUS *extremely wicked.*

54 OBNOXIOUS *liable (to anything harmful).*

55 be fair, young, and vegetous, no sweetmeats ever drew more flies;
all the yellow doublets and great roses i' the town will be there. If
foul and crooked, she'll be with them and buy those doublets and
roses, sir. If rich and that you marry her dowry, not her, she'll reign
in your house as imperious as a widow. If noble, all her kindred will
60 be your tyrants. If fruitful, as proud as May and humorous as April;
she must have her doctors, her midwives, her nurses, her longings
every hour, though it be for the dearest morsel of man. If learned,
there was never such a parrot; all your patrimony will be too little for
the guests that must be invited to hear her speak Latin and Greek,
65 and you must lie with her in those languages too, if you will please
her. If precise, you must feast all the silenced brethren, once in three
days; salute the sisters; entertain the whole family or wood of 'em;
and hear long-winded exercises, singings, and catechizings, which
you are not given to and yet must give for, to please the zealous
70 matron your wife, who for the holy cause will cozen you, over and
above. You begin to sweat, sir? But this is not half, i' faith; you
may do your pleasure notwithstanding, as I said before; I come not
to persuade you. Upon my faith, master servingman,   *The Mute is*
if you do stir, I will beat you.   *stealing away*

75   *Morose.* O, what is my sin! What is my sin?

Truewit. Then, if you love your wife, or rather dote on her, sir,
O, how she'll torture you and take pleasure i' your torments! You
shall lie with her but when she lists; she will not hurt her beauty,

---

55 VEGETOUS *healthy, vigorous (OED).*

56 DOUBLETS . . . ROSES *at once synecdoches of the gallant's dress and metonymies
of the courtier; "roses" were ribbons gathered into a rose-like knot and worn
on the front of a shoe (OED).*

60 HUMOROUS *capricious.*

66 PRECISE *puritanical.*

   SILENCED BRETHREN *those excommunicated for not complying with the canons
approved in 1604 by the Hampton Court Conference.*

67 WOOD *crowd or "forest" (after Latin* silva*); a favorite analogy of Jonson in
titling his works*—Timber, The Forest, Underwoods.

her complexion; or it must be for that jewel or that pearl when she does; every half hour's pleasure must be bought anew, and with the same pain and charge you wooed her at first. Then you must keep what servants she please, what company she will; that friend must not visit you without her license; and him she loves most she will seem to hate eagerliest, to decline your jealousy; or feign to be jealous of you first, and for that cause go live with her she-friend or cousin at the college, that can instruct her in all the mysteries of writing letters, corrupting servants, taming spies; where she must have that rich gown for such a great day, a new one for the next, a richer for the third; be served in silver; have the chamber filled with a succession of grooms, footmen, ushers, and other messengers, besides embroiderers, jewelers, tire-women, sempsters, feathermen, perfumers; while she feels not how the land drops away, nor the acres melt, nor foresees the change when the mercer has your woods for her velvets; never weighs what her pride costs, sir, so she may kiss a page or a smooth chin that has the despair of a beard; be a stateswoman, know all the news; what was done at Salisbury, what at the Bath, what at court, what in progress; or so she may censure poets and authors and styles, and compare 'em, Daniel with Spenser, Jonson with the t'other youth, and so forth; or be thought cunning in controversies or the very knots of divinity, and have often in her mouth the state of the question, and then skip to the

84 EAGERLIEST *most fiercely* (OED).
DECLINE *turn aside.*

85 SHE-FRIEND "*female friend, often in bad sense*" (OED).

86 COUSIN *a term of relationship or intimacy or contempt (in canting language, a "cousin" was a strumpet).*

91 TIRE-WOMEN *servants who assist at dressing.*
SEMPSTERS *men or women who sew.*
FEATHERMEN *dealers in feathers and plumes.*

93 MERCER *dealer in textiles, especially silks and velvets.*

96 STATESWOMAN *N.*

98–99 DANIEL . . . YOUTH *N.*

mathematics and demonstration, and answer, in religion to one, in
state to another, in bawdry to a third.

    Morose. O, O!

105   *Truewit.* All this is very true, sir. And then her going in disguise to
that conjurer and this cunning woman, where the first question is,
how soon you shall die? next, if her present servant love her? next
that, if she shall have a new servant? and how many? which of her
family would make the best bawd, male or female? what precedence
110 she shall have by her next match? And sets down the answers, and
believes 'em above the scriptures. Nay, perhaps she'll study the art.

    Morose. Gentle sir, ha' you done? Ha' you had your pleasure o'
me? I'll think of these things.

    Truewit. Yes, sir; and then comes reeking home of vapor and
115 sweat with going afoot, and lies in a month of a new face, all oil and
birdlime, and rises in asses' milk, and is cleansed with a new fucus.
God be w'you, sir. One thing more, which I had almost forgot.
This too, with whom you are to marry, may have made a conveyance of her virginity aforehand, as your wise widows do of their
120 states, before they marry, in trust to some friend, sir. Who can tell?
Or if she have not done it yet, she may do, upon the wedding day,
or the night before, and antedate you cuckold. The like has been
heard of in nature. 'Tis no devised, impossible thing, sir. God be

102 DEMONSTRATION *making evident by reasoning; here, because of its association
with mathematics, applied to concrete data.*

103 STATE *politics.*

106 CUNNING WOMAN *a fortuneteller (*OED*).*

107 SERVANT *lover devoted to the service of his mistress.*

109 PRECEDENCE *right of preceding others in ceremonies.*

115 LIES IN *lit., be brought to bed to give birth to a child.*

116 BIRDLIME *a sticky substance spread on twigs to catch birds.*
    RISES *N.*
    FUCUS *a wash or coloring for the face.*

118–19 CONVEYANCE *N.*

123 DEVISED *invented, feigned.*

w'you. I'll be bold to leave this rope with you, sir, for a remembrance. Farewell, Mute. [*Exit Truewit.*] 125

Morose. Come, ha' me to my chamber, but first shut the door. [*The horn again.*] O, shut the door, shut the door! Is he come again? [*Enter Cutbeard.*]

Cutbeard. 'Tis I, sir, your barber.

Morose. O, Cutbeard, Cutbeard, Cutbeard! Here has been a 130 cutthroat with me; help me into my bed and give me physic with thy counsel. [*Exeunt.*]

126 HA' ME *have me—i.e., lead or take me.*
131 PHYSIC *medicine.*

Act II Scene 3

[*Daw's house.*]
[*Enter Daw, Clerimont, Dauphine, Epicoene.*]

Daw. Nay, an' she will, let her refuse at her own charges; 'tis nothing to me, gentlemen. But she will not be invited to the like feasts or guests every day.

Clerimont. O, by no means, she may not refuse—[*Aside to her:*] to stay at home, if you love your reputation; 'slight, you are invited 5 thither o' purpose to be seen and laughed at by the lady of the college and her shadows. This trumpeter hath pro- *They dissuade* claimed you. *her, privately.*

Dauphine. You shall not go; let him be laughed at in your stead for not bringing you, and put him to his extemporal faculty of 10 fooling and talking loud to staisfy the company.

Clerimont. He will suspect us, talk aloud—Pray, Mistress Epicoene,

1 AT . . . CHARGES *and pay for it.*
7 SHADOWS *toadies; mimics* (OED).
   THIS TRUMPETER *Daw.*

let's see your verses; we have Sir John Daw's leave; do not conceal
your servant's merit and your own glories.

15 *Epicoene.* They'll prove my servant's glories if you have his leave
so soon.

Dauphine. His vainglories, lady!

Daw. Show 'em, show 'em, Mistress! I dare own 'em.

Epicoene. Judge you, what glories!

20 *Daw.* Nay, I'll read 'em myself, too: an author must recite his
own works. It is a madrigal of modesty.

> "Modest and fair, for fair and good are near
> Neighbors, howe'er"—

Dauphine. Very good.

25 *Clerimont.* Ay, is't not?

Daw. "No noble virtue ever was alone,
> But two in one."

Dauphine. Excellent!

Clerimont. That again, I pray, Sir John.

30 *Dauphine.* It has something in 't like rare wit and sense.

Clerimont. Peace.

Daw. "No noble virtue ever was alone,
> But two in one.
> Then, when I praise sweet modesty, I praise
35 > Bright beauty's rays:
> And having praised both beauty' and modestee,
> I have praised thee."

Dauphine. Admirable!

Clerimont. How it chimes and cries tink i' the close, divinely!

---

21 MADRIGAL *in general, lyric about love.*

22–37 NEAR . . . THEE *the rhymes—near/howe'er, alone/one, modestee/thee—
were perfectly good rhymes then, as Clerimont indicates by his ironic praise
of the verses as "chiming" in l. 39.*

39 CHIMES *jingles.*
CRIES TINK *tinkles.*

Dauphine. Ay, 'tis Seneca.   40

Clerimont. No, I think 'tis Plutarch.

Daw. The dor on Plutarch, and Seneca, I hate it! They are mine own imaginations, by that light. I wonder those fellows have such credit with gentlemen!

Clerimont. They are very grave authors.   45

Daw. Grave asses! Mere essayists! A few loose sentences, and that's all. A man would talk so his whole age; I do utter as good things every hour, if they were collected and observed, as either of 'em.

Dauphine. Indeed, Sir John!   50

Clerimont. He must needs, living among the Wits and Braveries too.

Dauphine. Ay, and being president of 'em as he is.

Daw. There's Aristotle, a mere commonplace fellow; Plato, a discourser; Thucydides and Livy, tedious and dry; Tacitus, an en-   55
tire knot, sometimes worth the untying, very seldom.

Clerimont. What do you think of the poets, Sir John?

Daw. Not worthy to be named for authors. Homer, an old, tedious, prolix ass, talks of curriers and chines of beef. Virgil, of dunging of land, and bees. Horace, of I know not what.   60

Clerimont. I think so.

Daw. And so Pindarus, Lycophron, Anacreon, Catullus, Seneca

40–41 SENECA . . . PLUTARCH *N.*

42 THE DOR ON *a scoffing dismissal, roughly, "the hell with."*

43 BY THAT LIGHT *exclamation referring originally to daylight; cf. variant, "by God's light," abbreviated as "'Slight."*

46 SENTENCES *maxims or sententious sayings.*

47 A MAN . . . AGE *anyone speaks as wisely as Seneca and Plutarch his whole life long.*

54–60 ARISTOTLE . . . HORACE *N.*

56 KNOT *tangle; "knotty problem."*

59–60 CURRIERS . . . BEES *N.*

CHINES *any part of the backbone, such as ribs or sirloin.*

62–64 PINDARUS . . . FLACCUS *N.*

the tragedian, Lucan, Propertius, Tibullus, Martial, Juvenal, Ausonius, Statius, Politian, Valerius Flaccus, and the rest—

65   *Clerimont.* What a sackful of their names he has got!

    Dauphine. And how he pours 'em out! Politian with Valerius
Flaccus!

    Clerimont. Was not the character right of him?

    Dauphine. As could be made, i' faith.

70   *Daw.* And Persius, a crabbed coxcomb not to be endured.

    Dauphine. Why, whom do you account for authors, Sir John
Daw?

    Daw. Syntagma juris civilis, Corpus juris civilis, Corpus juris canonici,
the King of Spain's Bible.

75   *Dauphine.* Is the King of Spain's Bible an author?

    Clerimont. Yes, and *Syntagma.*

    Dauphine. What was that *Syntagma,* sir?

    Daw. A civil lawyer, a Spaniard.

    Dauphine. Sure, *Corpus* was a Dutchman.

80   *Clerimont.* Ay, both the Corpuses, I knew 'em: they were very
corpulent authors.

    Daw. And then there's Vatablus, Pomponatius, Symancha; the
other are not to be received within the thought of a scholar.

    Dauphine. [*Aside.*] 'Fore God, you have a simple learned servant,
85 lady, in titles.

    Clerimont. I wonder that he is not called to the helm and made a
counsellor!

68 WAS . . . HIM *Didn't we describe his nature accurately (earlier, in I.2.60–78 and
I.3.15–20).*

70 PERSIUS *Aulus Persius Flaccus* (A.D. *34–62*), *a Roman poet whose satires often
seem obscure ("crabbed").*

73 SYNTAGMA . . . CANONICI *titles of collections of Roman Law, civil and canon.*
"Corpus" *means a general collection, and* "syntagma" *a systematic collection.*

75 KING OF SPAIN'S BIBLE *the polyglot Bible authorized by Philip II of Spain,
edited by Arias Montanus, and published at Antwerp, 1569–72.*

82 VATABLUS . . . SYMANCHA *N.*

Dauphine. He is one extraordinary.

Clerimont. Nay, but in ordinary! To say truth, the state wants such.   90

Dauphine. Why, that will follow.

Clerimont. I muse a mistress can be so silent to the dotes of such a servant.

Daw. 'Tis her virtue, sir. I have written somewhat of her silence too.   95

Dauphine. In verse, Sir John?

Clerimont. What else?

Dauphine. Why, how can you justify your own being of a poet, that so slight all the old poets?

Daw. Why, every man that writes in verse is not a poet; you have   100
of the Wits that write verses and yet are no poets; they are poets that live by it, the poor fellows that live by it.

Dauphine. Why, would not you live by your verses, Sir John?

Clerimont. No, 'twere pity he should. A knight live by his verses? He did not make 'em to that end, I hope.   105

Dauphine. And yet the noble Sidney lives by his, and the noble family not ashamed.

Clerimont. Ay, he professed himself; but Sir John Daw has more caution: he'll not hinder his own rising i' the state so much! Do you think he will? Your verses, good Sir John, and no poems.   110

Daw. "Silence in woman is like speech in man,
          Deny't who can."

Dauphine. Not I, believe it; your reason, sir.

110 and] are F₂, F₃.

89 IN ORDINARY *belonging to the regular staff; opposed to officials* "extraordinary."
    WANTS *an ironic play: lacks, requires.*
92 DOTES *natural gifts, but with the implication of dotage.*
99 POETS *N.*
106 SIDNEY *N.*

> Daw.   "Nor is't a tale
115   That female vice should be a virtue male,
>   Or masculine vice, a female virtue be:
>   You shall it see
>   Proved with increase,
>   I know to speak, and she to hold her peace."

120 Do you conceive me, gentlemen?

Dauphine. No, faith; how mean you "with increase," Sir John?

Daw. Why "with increase" is when I court her for the common cause of mankind, and she says nothing, but *consentire videtur*, and in time is *gravida*.

125 *Dauphine.* Then this is a ballad of procreation?

Clerimont. A madrigal of procreation; you mistake.

Epicoene. Pray give me my verses again, servant.

Daw. If you'll ask 'em aloud, you shall.

Clerimont. See here's Truewit again!

[Daw moves to one side, studying his verses.]

114–20 TALE ... CONCEIVE *Daw seems unaware of the sexual implications of such words as "tale," "increase," "peace," "conceive."*

121 INCREASE *becoming more numerous; offspring.*

123 CONSENTIRE VIDETUR *she seems to agree.*

124 GRAVIDA *pregnant.*

Act II Scene 4

[Enter Truewit with the post-horn.]

Clerimont. Where hast thou been, in the name of madness, thus accoutered with thy horn?

Truewit. Where the sound of it might have pierced your senses with gladness had you been in ear-reach of it. Dauphine, fall down

and worship me; I have forbid the banns, lad. I have been with thy   5
virtuous uncle and have broke the match.

Dauphine. You ha' not, I hope.

Truewit. Yes, faith, an' thou shouldst hope otherwise, I should
repent me; this horn got me entrance, kiss it. I had no other way to
get in but by feigning to be a post; but when I got in once, I proved   10
none, but rather the contrary, turned him into a post or a stone or
what is stiffer, with thundering into him the incommodities of a wife
and the miseries of marriage. If ever Gorgon were seen in the shape
of a woman, he hath seen her in my description. I have put him off
o' that scent forever. Why do you not applaud and adore me, sirs?   15
Why stand you mute? Are you stupid? You are not worthy o' the
benefit.

Dauphine. Did not I tell you? Mischief!—

Clerimont. I would you had placed this benefit somewhere else.

Truewit. Why so?   20

Clerimont. 'Slight, you have done the most inconsiderate, rash,
weak thing that ever man did to his friend.

Dauphine. Friend! If the most malicious enemy I have, had studied
to inflict an injury upon me, it could not be a greater.

Truewit. Wherein, for God's sake? Gentlemen, come to your-   25
selves again.

Dauphine. But I presaged thus much afore to you.

Clerimont. Would my lips had been soldered when I spake on 't.
'Slight, what moved you to be thus impertinent?

Truewit. My masters, do not put on this strange face to pay my   30

---

5 WORSHIP *venerate, do honor to. See* "adore," *l. 15.*
   HAVE FORBID THE BANNS *made a formal objection to an intended marriage.*
13 GORGON *one of the three mythical female beings, with snakes for hair, whose
look turned the beholder into stone; Medusa was the most famous. See* III.7.20.
16 STUPID *stupified.*
30 PUT . . . FACE *affect a cold, estranged manner.*

courtesy; off with this visor. Have good turns done you and thank 'em this way?

    Dauphine. 'Fore heav'n, you have undone me. That which I have plotted for and been maturing now these four months, you have
35 blasted in a minute. Now I am lost, I may speak. This gentlewoman was lodged here by me o' purpose, and, to be put upon my uncle, hath professed this obstinate silence for my sake, being my entire friend, and one that for the requital of such a fortune as to marry him, would have made me very ample conditions; where now all
40 my hopes are utterly miscarried by this unlucky accident.

    Clerimont. Thus 'tis, when a man will be ignorantly officious, do services, and not know his why. I wonder what courteous itch possessed you! You never did absurder part i' your life, nor a greater trespass to friendship, to humanity.

45   *Dauphine.* Faith, you may forgive it best; 'twas your cause principally.

    Clerimont. I know it; would it had not.

[Enter Cutbeard.]

    Dauphine. How now, Cutbeard, what news?

    Cutbeard. The best, the happiest that ever was, sir. There has been
50 a mad gentleman with your uncle this morning [*seeing Truewit*]— I think this be the gentleman—that has almost talked him out of his wits with threatening him from marriage—

    Dauphine. On, I pray thee.

    Cutbeard. And your uncle, sir, he thinks 'twas done by your
55 procurement; therefore he will see the party you wot of presently, and if he like her, he says, and that she be so inclining to dumb as I have told him, he swears he will marry her today, instantly, and not defer it a minute longer.

---

36 TO . . . UPON *two senses coincide: to trick, by being imposed upon him.*

55 PRESENTLY *immediately, without any delay.*

56 TO DUMB *to be dumb.*

Dauphine. Excellent! Beyond our expectation!

Truewit. Beyond your expectation? By this light, I knew it would   60
be thus.

Dauphine. Nay, sweet Truewit, forgive me.

Truewit. No, I was "ignorantly officious, impertinent"; this was
the "absurd, weak part."

Clerimont. Wilt thou ascribe that to merit now, was mere fortune?   65

Truewit. Fortune? Mere providence. Fortune had not a finger in
't. I saw it must necessarily in nature fall out so: my genius is never
false to me in these things. Show me how it could be otherwise.

Dauphine. Nay, gentlemen, contend not; 'tis well now.

Truewit. Alas, I let him go on with "inconsiderate" and "rash"   70
and what he pleased

Clerimont. Away, thou strange justifier of thyself, to be wiser
than thou wert by the event.

Truewit. Event! By this light, thou shalt never persuade me but I
foresaw it as well as the stars themselves.   75

Dauphine. Nay, gentlemen, 'tis well now. Do you two entertain Sir John Daw with discourse while I send her away with
instructions.

Truewit. I'll be acquainted with her first, by your favor.

Clerimont. Master Truewit, lady, a friend of ours.   80

Truewit. I am sorry I have not known you sooner, lady, to
celebrate this rare virtue of your silence.

---

60 BY THIS LIGHT *see II.3.43 and fn.*

65 WAS *which was.*

66 FORTUNE *Truewit makes a conventional distinction between chance or luck,
regarded as a cause of events, and divine providence—the foreknowing care of God
or nature.*

MERE *nothing short of.*

67 GENIUS *attendant spirit allotted to a person at birth, to govern his fortunes and
determine his character.*

73 EVENT *outcome.*

Act II Scene 4

Clerimont. Faith, an' you had come sooner, you should ha' seen and heard her well celebrated in Sir John Daw's "madrigals."

[*Exeunt Dauphine, Epicoene, and Cutbeard, as Truewit approaches Daw.*]

85   *Truewit.* Jack Daw, God save you, when saw you La Foole?

Daw. Not since last night, Master Truewit.

Truewit. That's miracle! I thought you two had been inseparable.

Daw. He's gone to invite his guests.

Truewit. Gods so, 'tis true! What a false memory have I towards
90 that man! I am one: I met him e'en now upon that he calls his delicate fine black horse, rid into a foam with posting from place to place and person to person to give 'em the cue—

Clerimont. Lest they should forget?

Truewit. Yes, There was never poor captain took more pains at a
95 muster to show men than he, at this meal, to show friends.

Daw. It is his quarter-feast, sir.

Clerimont. What! Do you say so, Sir John?

Truewit. Nay, Jack Daw will not be out, at the best friends he has, to the talent of his wit. Where's his mistress to hear and applaud him?
100 Is she gone?

Daw. Is Mistress Epicoene gone?

Clerimont. Gone afore with Sir Dauphine, I warrant, to the place.

Truewit. Gone afore! That were a manifest injury, a disgrace and a half, to refuse him at such a festival time as this, being a Bravery
105 and a Wit too.

87 that's miracle] that's a miracle F₂, F₃.

---

89 GODS SO *variant of* "catso" (*from Italian* cazzo, penis), *as exclamation; sometimes term of contempt; see IV.2.23.*

90 ONE *one of the guests.*

96 QUARTER-FEAST *a feast celebrating Quarter-day, one of four days marking off the quarters of the year. N.*

98–99 OUT . . . TALENT *i.e., Daw will not abstain from a display of his wit even at the cost of his best friends.*

Clerimont. Tut, he'll swallow it like cream. He's better read in *jure civili* than to esteem anything a disgrace is offered him from a mistress.

Daw. Nay, let her e'en go; she shall sit alone and be dumb in her chamber a week together, for John Daw, I warrant her. Does she refuse me? 110

Clerimont. No, sir, do not take it so to heart; she does not refuse you but a little neglect you. Good faith, Truewit, you were to blame to put it into his head that she does refuse him.

Truewit. She does refuse him, sir, palpably, however you mince 115 it. An' I were as he, I would swear to speak ne'er a word to her to-day for't.

Daw. By this light, no more I will not.

Truewit. Nor to anybody else, sir.

Daw. Nay, I will not say so, gentlemen. 120

Clerimont. [*Aside.*] It had been an excellent happy condition for the company if you could have drawn him to it.

Daw. I'll be very melancholic, i' faith.

Clerimont. As a dog, if I were as you, Sir John.

Truewit. Or a snail or a hog-louse. I would roll myself up for 125 this day; in troth, they should not unwind me.

Daw. By this picktooth, so I will.

Clerimont. [*Aside.*] 'Tis well done: he begins already to be angry with his teeth.

---

107 JURE CIVILI *civil law. See II.3.73.*

　　DISGRACE IS *disgrace that is.*

115 MINCE *make little of.*

125 HOG-LOUSE *woodlouse.*

　　ROLL MYSELF UP *Daw is associated with coiled forms of lower life: characteristically, the woodlouse rolls itself into a ball; the snail has a spiral shell into which it can withdraw; and the dog sleeps coiled up after thrice circling around its resting place.*

127 PICKTOOTH *toothpick; often affected by gallants of the age and evidently flourished by Daw.*

130　*Daw*. Will you go, gentlemen?

Clerimont. Nay, you must walk alone, if you be right melancholic, Sir John.

Truewit. Yes, sir, we'll dog you, we'll follow you afar off. [*Exit Daw*.]

135　*Clerimont*. Was there ever such a two yards of knighthood, measured out by time, to be sold to laughter?

Truewit. A mere talking mole! Hang him, no mushroom was ever so fresh. A fellow so utterly nothing, as he knows not what he would be.

140　*Clerimont*. Let's follow him, but first let's go to Dauphine; he's hovering about the house to hear what news.

Truewit. Content. [*Exeunt*.]

131　MELANCHOLIC *walking alone was thought to be a sign of melancholy brought on by frustrated love.*

137　MOLE *because of his blindness? (See ll. 138–39). Curiously, there is a mole hog-louse* (Apsendes talpa), *though Jonson may not have known this (see l. 125).*

MUSHROOM *Jonson habitually thought of new knights as fungi—"mushrompe gentlemen, / That shoot vp in a night to place, and worship"* (Every Man Out, I.2.162–63).

Act II Scene 5

[*Morose's house*.]

[*Enter Morose and Mute, followed by Cutbeard with Epicoene*.]

Morose. Welcome, Cutbeard! Draw near with your fair charge, and, in her ear, softly entreat her to unmask.

[*Cutbeard whispers to Epicoene, who removes her mask*.]

So. Is the door shut? [*Mute makes a leg*.]—enough. Now, Cutbeard

with the same discipline I use to my family, I will question you. As I
conceive, Cutbeard, this gentlewoman is she you have provided   5
and brought, in hope she will fit me in the place and person of a wife?
Answer me not but with your leg, unless it be otherwise—[*Cutbeard
makes a leg*]—very well done, Cutbeard. I conceive besides, Cutbeard, you have been pre-acquainted with her birth, education, and
qualities, or else you would not prefer her to my acceptance, in the   10
weighty consequence of marriage—[*Makes a leg*]—this I conceive,
Cutbeard. Answer me not but with your leg, unless it be otherwise
—[*Makes a leg again*] Very well done, Cutbeard. Give aside now a
little and leave me to examine her condition and aptitude to my
affection. She is exceeding fair and of a special good   *He goes about*   15
favor; a sweet composition or harmony of limbs; her   *her, and views
her.*
temper of beauty has the true height of my blood. The knave hath
exceedingly well fitted me without; I will now try her within.
Come near, fair gentlewoman; let not my behavior seem rude,
though unto you, being rare, it may haply appear strange. *She*   20
curtsies. Nay, lady, you may speak, though Cutbeard and my man
might not: for of all sounds only the sweet voice of a fair lady has
the just length of mine ears. I beseech you, say, lady; out of the first
fire of meeting eyes, they say, love is stricken: do you feel any such
motion suddenly shot into you from any part you see in me? Ha,   25
lady?—*Curtsy.*—Alas, lady, these answers by silent curtsies, from
you, are too courtless and simple. I have ever had my breeding in

---

4 FAMILY *the servants of the house.* Latin familia = *household.*

16 FAVOR *appearance; attractiveness.*

16–17 HER . . . BLOOD *presumably, the exact balance of features that most arouses
his passion; see Introduction, p. 9. "Temper" suggests both a musical image
("composition," "harmony") and the traditional belief that temperament is
determined by the combination of the four bodily "humours."*

23 JUST LENGTH OF "*attuned to, as is the string of a viol*" (*Beaurline*).

27 COURTLESS *uncourtly, i.e., not fitting the fantasies defined in ll. 41 ff. and
61 ff. below.*

court, and she that shall be my wife must be accomplished with courtly and audacious ornaments. Can you speak, lady?

30   *Epicoene.* Judge you, forsooth. [*She speaks softly.*]

   Morose. What say you, lady? Speak out, I beseech you.

   Epicoene. Judge you, forsooth.

   Morose. O' my judgment, a divine softness! But can you naturally, lady, as I enjoin these by doctrine and industry, refer yourself to the

35 search of my judgment and, not taking pleasure in your tongue, which is a woman's chiefest pleasure, think it plausible to answer me by silent gestures, so long as my speeches jump right with what you conceive?—*Curtsy.*—Excellent! Divine! If it were possible she should hold out thus! Peace, Cutbeard, thou art made forever, as

40 thou hast made me, if this felicity have lasting; but I will try her further. Dear lady, I am courtly, I tell you, and I must have mine ears banqueted with pleasant and witty conferences, pretty girds, scoffs, and dalliance in her that I mean to choose for my bed-fere. The ladies in court think it a most desperate impair to their quick-

45 ness of wit, and good carriage, if they cannot give occasion for a man to court 'em, and when an amorous discourse is set on foot, minister

---

29 AUDACIOUS *he means "self-confident" but other meanings threaten: e.g., "defiant of decorum" (OED).*

34 ENJOIN *prescribe authoritatively: "more authoritative than 'direct,' and less imperious than 'command'" (Samuel Johnson,* A Dictionary of the English Language, *4th ed. [London, 1773]).*
   THESE *Cutbeard and the servant.*

35 SEARCH . . . JUDGMENT *extent to which my judgment reaches.*

36 PLAUSIBLE *pleasing.*

37 JUMP . . . WITH *agree completely with.*

40 LASTING *duration.*

42 GIRDS *jibes, biting remarks.*

43 BED–FERE *bedfellow.*

44 IMPAIR *injury.*

45 CARRIAGE *behavior, bearing.*

46 MINISTER *supply.*

as good matter to continue it as himself; and do you alone so much differ from all them, that what they, with so much circumstance, affect and toil for, to seem learned, to seem judicious, to seem sharp and conceited, you can bury in yourself with silence? and rather   50
trust your graces to the fair conscience of virtue than to the world's or your own proclamation?

Epicoene. I should be sorry else.

Morose. What say you, lady? Good lady, speak out.

Epicoene. I should be sorry, else.   55

Morose. That sorrow doth fill me with gladness! O Morose, thou art happy above mankind! Pray that thou mayst contain thyself. I will only put her to it once more, and it shall be with the utmost touch and test of their sex. But hear me, fair lady; I do also love to see her whom I shall choose for my heifer to be the first and principal   60
in all fashions, precede all the dames at court by a fortnight, have her council of tailors, lineners, lace-women, embroiderers, and sit with 'em sometimes twice a day upon French intelligences, and then come forth varied like Nature, or oftener than she, and better by the help of Art, her emulous servant. This do I affect. And how will you   65
be able, lady, with this frugality of speech, to give the manifold—but necessary—instructions for that bodice, these sleeves, those skirts,

60 heifer] heicfar F.

---

48 CIRCUMSTANCE *ceremony as in* "*pomp and circumstance.*"

50 CONCEITED *witty.*

51 CONSCIENCE *inward knowledge.*

59 TOUCH *test, proof.*

60 HEIFER *the expression is rude to Epicoene, but ominous for Morose if, as H & S suggest, it derives from the story of the treacherous wife who enticed Samson to break his silence and disclose the answer to the riddle of the lion and honey:* "*If ye had not plowed with my heifer, ye had not found out my riddle*" (Judges *14:18*).

62 LINENERS *sellers of linens; shirtmakers.*

62–63 SIT . . . INTELLIGENCES *deliberate on news (of fashion) from France.*

this cut, that stitch, this embroidery, that lace, this wire, those knots, that ruff, those roses, this girdle, that fan, the t'other scarf, these
70 gloves? Ha? What say you, lady?

    Epicoene. I'll leave it to you, sir.

    Morose. How, lady? Pray you, rise a note.

    Epicoene. I leave it to wisdom and you, sir.

    Morose. Admirable creature! I will trouble you no more. I will not
75 sin against so sweet a simplicity. Let me now be bold to print on those divine lips the seal of being mine. [*Kisses her.*] Cutbeard, I give thee the lease of thy house free; thank me not, but with thy leg— [*Cutbeard makes a gesture of protest*]—I know what thou wouldst say, she's poor and her friends deceased; she has brought a wealthy dowry
80 in her silence, Cutbeard, and in respect of her poverty, Cutbeard, I shall have her more loving and obedient, Cutbeard. Go thy ways and get me a minister presently, with a soft, low voice to marry us, and pray him he will not be impertinent, but brief as he can; away, softly, Cutbeard. [*Exit Cutbeard.*] Sirrah, conduct your mistress into
85 the dining room, your now-mistress. O my felicity! [*Exeunt Mute How I shall be revenged on mine insolent kinsman and Epicene.*] and his plots to fright me from marrying! This night I will get an heir and thrust him out of my blood like a stranger; he would be knighted, forsooth, and thought by that means to reign over me,
90 his title must do it. No, kinsman, I will now make you bring me the

68 CUT *probably, the slashes made in gowns through which the silk might show; possibly, the general cut or shape of a garment.*
    WIRE *a frame of wire to support the hair or the ruff. See* Prologue, *l. 23 and fn.*
69 RUFF *neckwear of starched linen or muslin arranged in horizontal flutings.*
    ROSES *see II.2.58.*
    GIRDLE *then a belt worn round the waist to confine the garments.*
83 IMPERTINENT *irrelevant.*
85–113 N.
88 BLOOD *blood-relationship or lineage. Morose's extravagance again: he cannot change the blood-relationship with Dauphine by begetting a child; he can only keep Dauphine from being his legal heir.*

tenth lord's and the sixteenth lady's letter, kinsman, and it shall do
you no good, kinsman. Your knighthood itself shall come on its
knees, and it shall be rejected; it shall be sued for its fees to execution,
and not be redeemed; it shall cheat at the twelve-penny ordinary, it
knighthood, for its diet all the term time, and tell tales for it in the   95
vacation to the hostess; or it knighthood shall do worse, take
sanctuary in Coleharbour, and fast. It shall fright all it friends with
borrowing letters, and when one of the fourscore hath brought it
knighthood ten shillings, it knighthood shall go to the Cranes or
the Bear at the Bridge-foot and be drunk in fear; it shall not have   100
money to discharge one tavern-reckoning, to invite the old creditors
to forbear it knighthood, or the new that should be, to trust it
knighthood. It shall be the tenth name in the bond, to take up the
commodity of pipkins and stone jugs, and the part thereof shall not
furnish it knighthood forth for the attempting of a baker's widow, a   105

---

91 TENTH LORD'S . . . LETTER *letters attesting to Dauphine's character or his*
acceptability in aristocratic society?
93 EXECUTION *enforcement by the sheriff of the judgment of the court; here, apparently*
seizure of goods in default of payment of debts.
94 ORDINARY *originally, a meal regularly provided in a tavern; later, also the*
eating-house where such meals were provided. Often one could gamble there
too: hence "cheat."
IT *possessive its; an archaic form used contemptuously throughout this passage.*
95 DIET *food.*
TERM *see I.1.46.*
TELL . . . IT *i.e., get free meals by amusing the hostess with stories.*
96 VACATION *period during which law courts were closed.*
97 COLEHARBOUR *or Cold Harborough, a sanctuary for debtors and vagrants on*
Upper Thames Street.
99–100 CRANES . . . BEAR *popular taverns in London.*
BRIDGE-FOOT *i.e., of London Bridge.*
104 COMMODITY *N.*
PIPKINS *small earthenware pots.*
105 FURNISH . . . FORTH *equip the knight.*
ATTEMPTING OF *trying to seduce.*

brown baker's widow. It shall give it knighthood's name for a stallion to all gamesome citizens' wives and be refused, when the master of a dancing school, or—how do you call him?—the worst reveller in the town is taken; it shall want clothes, and by reason of
110 that, wit, to fool to lawyers. It shall not have hope to repair itself by Constantinople, Ireland, or Virginia; but the best and last fortune to it knighthood shall be to make Dol Tearsheet or Kate Common a lady, and so it knighthood may eat. [*Exit.*]

106 BROWN BAKER'S *baker of coarse and inferior bread.*
108 HOW *N.*
109 TAKEN *accepted as a lover ("stallion," ll. 111–12).*
110 FOOL TO *delude.*
111 CONSTANTINOPLE . . . VIRGINIA *Morose mentions three places where younger brothers, wastrels, and criminals could go to rescue their fortunes or escape the law.*
112–13 TO MAKE . . . MAY EAT *to make Dol or Kate (types of whores, the first from Shakespeare's* 2 Henry IV, *the second from colloquial speech) a lady by marrying her and then to live off her earnings.*

Act II Scene 6

[*A lane near Morose's house.*]
[*Enter Truewit, Dauphine, and Clerimont.*]
Truewit. Are you sure he is not gone by?
Dauphine. No, I stayed in the shop ever since.
Clerimont. But he may take the other end of the lane.
Dauphine. No, I told him I would be here at this end; I appointed
5 him hither.
Truewit. What a barbarian it is to stay then!

1 HE *Cutbeard.*
4–5 APPOINTED HIM HITHER *made an appointment for a meeting with him here.*
6 IT *i.e., he.*

Dauphine. Yonder he comes.

Clerimont. And his charge left behind him, which is a very good sign, Dauphine.

[Enter Cutbeard.]

Dauphine. How now, Cutbeard, succeeds it or no?　　　10

Cutbeard. Past imagination, sir, *omnia secunda;* you could not have prayed to have had it so well. *Saltat senex,* as it is i' the proverb; he does triumph in his felicity, admires the party! He has given me the lease of my house too! And I am now going for a silent minister to marry 'em, and away.　　　15

Truewit. 'Slight, get one o' the silenced ministers; a zealous brother would torment him purely.

Cutbeard. Cum privilegio, sir.

Dauphine. O, by no means; let's do nothing to hinder it now; when 'tis done and finished, I am for you, for any device of vexation.　　20

Cutbeard. And that shall be within this half hour, upon my dexterity, gentlemen. Contrive what you can in the meantime, *bonis avibus.* [Exit.]

Clerimont. How the slave doth Latin it!

Truewit. It would be made a jest to posterity, sirs, this day's mirth,　　25 if ye will.

Clerimont. Beshrew his heart that will not, I pronounce.

Dauphine. And for my part. What is't?

11–12 OMNIA . . . SENEX *"All is well, the old man dances"—a Roman proverb.*

16 SILENCED MINISTERS *see II.2.66 and fn.*

17 PURELY *perfectly; with a quibble on Puritans, some of whom were "silenced brethren."*

18 CUM PRIVILEGIO *with exclusive right (privileged as a minister to produce a sermon even at a wedding).*

22–23 BONIS AVIBUS *with good omens.*

25 JEST *note that Clerimont and Dauphine agree to take part in Truewit's jest before finding out what it is.*

27 BESHREW *a curse on; devil take!*

Act II Scene 6

Truewit. To translate all La Foole's company and his feast hither
30   today, to celebrate this bridal.

Dauphine. Ay, marry, but how will't be done?

Truewit. I'll undertake the directing of all the lady guests thither,
and then the meat must follow.

Clerimont. For God's sake, let's effect it; it will be an excellent
35   comedy of affliction, so many several noises.

Dauphine. But are they not at the other place already, think you?

Truewit. I'll warrant you for the college-honors: one o' their faces
has not the priming color laid on yet, nor the other her smock
sleeked.

40   *Clerimont.* O, but they'll rise earlier than ordinary to a feast.

Truewit. Best go see, and assure ourselves.

Clerimont. Who knows the house?

Truewit. I'll lead you. Were you never there yet?

Dauphine. Not I.

45   *Clerimont.* Nor I.

Truewit. Where ha' you lived then? Not know Tom Otter!

Clerimont. No. For God's sake, what is he?

Truewit. An excellent animal, equal with your Daw or La Foole,
if not transcendent, and does Latin it as much as your barber. He is
50   his wife's subject; he calls her Princess, and at such times as these
follows her up and down the house like a page, with his hat off,
partly for heat, partly for reverence. At this instant he is marshalling
of his bull, bear, and horse.

---

29   TRANSLATE *1. transfer. 2. transform (echoing the idea of metamorphosing)*.

30   BRIDAL *wedding or wedding feast*. N.

33   MEAT *food; feast*.

35   SEVERAL *individually separate; different*.

36   AT THE OTHER PLACE *the Otters'*.

37   WARRANT . . . COLLEGE-HONORS *guarantee this about the collegiate ladies*.

39   SLEEKED *made smooth or sleek, apparently by ironing*.

Dauphine. What be those, in the name of Sphinx?

Truewit. Why, sir, he has been a great man at the Bear Garden 55
in his time, and from that subtle sport has ta'en the witty denomination of his chief carousing cups. One he calls his bull, another his bear, another his horse, And then he has his lesser glasses, that he calls his deer and his ape, and several degrees of 'em too, and never is well, nor thinks any entertainment perfect, till these be brought 60
out and set o' the cupboard.

Clerimont. For God's love, we should miss this if we should not go!

Truewit. Nay, he has a thousand things as good that will speak him all day. He will rail on his wife, with certain commonplaces, behind her back, and to her face— 65

Dauphine. No more of him. Let's go see him, I petition you. [*Exeunt.*]

54 SPHINX *invoked because a propounder of riddles.*

55 BEAR GARDEN *N.*

57 CUPS *probably the covers would represent the heads of the animals. See the "bull-head" in IV.2.129–30.*

60 WELL *contented.*

63 SPEAK *show; describe.*

Act III Scene 1

[*Otter's house.*]
[*Enter Mistress Otter and Captain Otter with his cups.*]
Otter. Nay, good Princess, hear me *pauca verba.*

Mrs. Otter. By that light, I'll ha' you chained up with your
bull-dogs and bear-dogs, if you be not civil the sooner. I'll send you
to kennel, i'faith. You were best bait me with your bull, bear, and

5 horse! Never a time that the courtiers or collegiates come to the house,
but you make it a Shrove Tuesday! I would have you get your
Whitsuntide velvet cap and your staff i' your hand to entertain 'em;
yes, in troth, do.

Otter. Not so, Princess, neither; but under correction, sweet Prin-
10 cess, gi' me leave—these things I am known to the courtiers by. It is
reported to them for my humour, and they receive it so, and do
expect it. Tom Otter's bull, bear, and horse is known all over
England, in *rerum natura.*

1 PAUCA VERBA *few words; Otter is simply trying to get a word in, but the phrase
is proverbial: "few words to the wise suffice."*

4 YOU . . . BEST *you had best.* N.

6 SHROVE TUESDAY *see I.1.143.*

7 WHITSUNTIDE *N.*

9 UNDER CORRECTION *an expression of deference to superior authority.*

11 HUMOUR *temperamental oddity; here an affectation of eccentricity. See* Every
Man Out of his Humour, *the* Induction.

13 RERUM NATURA *literally, "the nature of things;" i.e., in all creation.* N.

Mrs. Otter. Fore me, I will "na-ture" 'em over to Paris Garden and "na-ture" you thither too, if you pronounce 'em again. Is a bear 15
a fit beast, or a bull, to mix in society with great ladies? Think i' your discretion, in any good polity?

Otter. The horse then, good Princess.

Mrs. Otter. Well, I am contented for the horse; they love to be well horsed, I know. I love it myself. 20

Otter. And it is a delicate fine horse this. *Poetarum Pegasus.* Under correction, Princess, Jupiter did turn himself into a—*Taurus* or bull, under correction, good Princess.

[*Truewit, Clerimont, and Dauphine enter, unnoticed.*]

Mrs. Otter. By my integrity, I'll send you over to the Bank-side; I'll commit you to the master of the Garden, if I hear but a syllable 25
more. Must my house, or my roof, be polluted with the scent of bears and bulls when it is perfumed for great ladies? Is this according to the instrument when I married you? That I would be Princess and reign in mine own house, and you would be my subject and obey me? What did you bring me, should make you thus peremp- 30
tory? Do I allow you your half-crown a day to spend, where you will, among your gamesters, to vex and torment me at such times as these? Who gives you your maintenance, I pray you? Who allows you your horse-meat and man's meat? your three suits of apparel a year? your four pair of stockings, one silk, three worsted? your 35

14 FORE *prep.* ("*for*") *in oaths, solemn affirmations, as* "*Fore God*"; *often spelled* "'*fore*" *as if shortened from* "*before*" (*OED*).

17 ANY . . . POLITY *civil or social order generally* (*not only that of* "*great ladies*").

21 POETARUM PEGASUS "*the Poets' Pegasus*": *the mythological winged horse as symbol of poetic inspiration.* N.

27 PERFUMED *not merely an exotic pleasure, considering the plumbing of the time.*

28 INSTRUMENT *legal document; here the marriage contract, summarized in the following lines. See Introduction, pp. 10–14.*

34 HORSE-MEAT *provender for horses—but just barely distinguishable from food for Otter.*

35 THREE . . . WORSTED *N.*

77

clean linen, your bands and cuffs, when I can get you to wear 'em? 'Tis mar'l you ha' 'em on now. Who graces you with courtiers or great personages, to speak to you out of their coaches, and come home to your house? Were you ever so much as looked upon by a
40 lord, or a lady, before I married you, but on the Easter or Whitsun holidays, and then out at the Banqueting-House windore, when Ned Whiting or George Stone were at the stake?

   Truewit. [*Aside.*] For God's sake, let's go stave her off him.

   Mrs. Otter. Answer me to that. And did not I take you up from
45 thence in an old greasy buff-doublet, with points, and green velvet sleeves, out at the elbows? You forget this.

   Truewit. [*Aside.*] She'll worry him, if we help not in time.
                    [*They come forward.*]

   Mrs. Otter. O, here are some o' the gallants! Go to, behave yourself distinctly, and with good morality, or I protest, I'll take
50 away your exhibition.

   36 BANDS *neckbands or collars of shirts.*
   37 MAR'L *marvel.*
   41 BANQUETING-HOUSE *at Whitehall, one of the King's residences, where royal entertainments were held.*
   41–42 NED . . . STONE *bears, which generally carried the names of their owners; the second, especially famous, was killed at Court in 1606.*
   43 STAVE *drive off with a staff, as dogs in bear- or bull-baiting.*
   45 BUFF-DOUBLET *a close-fitting jacket of leather ("buff") commonly worn by bailiffs and soldiers of low rank.*
      POINTS *laces, here presumably to fasten armor to the doublet, and thus the mark of a soldier.*
   47 WORRY *kill or injure by biting; said of hounds when they seize their quarry.*
   49 DISTINCTLY *mistake for "distinctively"; i.e., with discrimination? or, in a distinguished manner?*
   50 EXHIBITION *allowance of money.*

Act III Scene 2

Truewit. By your leave, fair Mistress Otter, I'll be bold to enter these gentlemen in your acquaintance.

Mrs. Otter. It shall not be obnoxious or difficil, sir.

Truewit. How does my noble Captain? Is the bull, bear, and horse in *rerum natura* still?   5

Otter. Sir, *sic visum superis.*

Mrs. Otter. I would you would but intimate 'em, do. Go your ways in, and get toasts and butter made for the woodcocks. That's a fit province for you. [*Chasing him out.*]

Clerimont. Alas, what a tyranny is this poor fellow married to!   10

Truewit. O, but the sport will be anon, when we get him loose.

Dauphine. Dares he ever speak?

Truewit. No Anabaptist ever railed with the like license; but mark her language in the meantime, I beseech you.

Mrs. Otter. Gentlemen, you are very aptly come. My cousin, Sir   15
Amorous, will be here briefly.

Truewit. In good time, lady. Was not Sir John Daw here, to ask for him and the company?

Mrs. Otter. I cannot assure you, Master Truewit. Here was a very

3 OBNOXIOUS OR DIFFICIL *offensive or troublesome; Mrs. Otter's affectation of what she thinks is courtly idiom.*

5 RERUM NATURA *in existence; see above, III.1.13, fn. and N.*

6 SIC . . . SUPERIS *as those above decree. N.*

7 INTIMATE *mistake for "imitate"? or "make yourself intimate with them"?*

8 WOODCOCKS *easily snared, this bird became a type of gullibility; hence, fool.*

13 ANABAPTIST *more a loose term of opprobrium applied to any radical Protestant zealot than an exact designation of the sect which advocated re-baptism of adults.*

16 BRIEFLY *soon.*

20   melancholy knight in a ruff, that demanded my subject for somebody, a gentleman, I think.

    Clerimont. Ay, that was he, lady.

    Mrs. Otter. But he departed straight, I can resolve you.

    Dauphine. What an excellent choice phrase this lady expresses in!

25   *Truewit.* O, sir, she is the only authentical courtier that is not
naturally bred one, in the city.

    Mrs. Otter. You have taken that report upon trust, gentlemen.

    Truewit. No, I assure you, the court governs it so, lady, in your
behalf.

30   *Mrs. Otter.* I am the servant of the court and courtiers, sir.

    Truewit. They are rather your idolaters.

    Mrs. Otter. Not so, sir.

                [Enter Cutbeard; they converse apart.]

    Dauphine. How now, Cutbeard? Any cross?

    Cutbeard. O, no, sir, *omnia bene.* 'Twas never better o' the hinges,

35   all's sure. I have so pleased him with a curate that he's gone to't almost with the delight he hopes for soon.

    Dauphine. What is he for a vicar?

    Cutbeard. One that has catched a cold, sir, and can scarce be heard
six inches off, as if he spoke out of a bulrush that were not picked, or

40   his throat were full of pith; a fine quick fellow and an excellent

20 SUBJECT *i.e., Otter.*

23 STRAIGHT *immediately.*

   RESOLVE *an affected way of saying "inform."*

28 GOVERNS *decides, determines.*

33 CROSS *thwarting; trouble.*

34 OMNIA BENE *all's well.*

   O' THE HINGES *the opposite of "off the hinges," which means "unhinged,"
"out of order" (H & S).*

37 WHAT . . . VICAR *what sort of vicar is he; compare the German "Was ist das
für ein . . .".*

39 BULRUSH . . . PICKED *N.*

barber of prayers. I came to tell you, sir, that you might *omnem movere lapidem*, as they say, be ready with your vexation.

Dauphine. Gramercy, honest Cutbeard, be thereabouts with thy key to let us in.

Cutbeard. I will not fail you, sir. *Ad manum.* [*Exit Cutbeard.*]   45

Truewit. Well, I'll go watch my coaches.

Clerimont. Do, and we'll send Daw to you if you meet him not.
[*Exit Truewit.*]

Mrs. Otter. Is Master Truewit gone?

Dauphine. Yes, lady, there is some unfortunate business fallen out.

Mrs. Otter. So I judged by the physiognomy of the fellow that   50
came in; and I had a dream last night too of the new pageant and
my Lady Mayoress, which is always very ominous to me. I told it
my Lady Haughty t'other day, when her honor came hither to see
some China stuffs, and she expounded it out of Artemidorus, and I
have found it since very true. It has done me many affronts.   55

Clerimont. Your dream, lady?

Mrs. Otter. Yes, sir, anything I do but dream o' the city. It
stained me a damask tablecloth, cost me eighteen pounds at one
time; and burnt me a black satin gown, as I stood by the fire at my
Lady Centaure's chamber in the college another time. A third time,   60
at the Lords' masque, it dropped all my wire and my ruff with wax
candle, that I could not go up to the banquet. A fourth time, as I was

41–42 OMNEM MOVERE LAPIDEM *leave no stone unturned.*

43 GRAMERCY *thanks (as in French "merci").*

45 AD MANUM *in hand: "I'm all ready."*

49 FALLEN OUT *happened.*

51 DREAM . . . PAGEANT *N.*

54 ARTEMIDORUS *a second-century Greek physician who wrote a long work on the interpretation of dreams.*

57 ANYTHING . . . CITY *if I dream anything at all about the city(?) I do little else but dream of the city(?)*
IT *probably the city. N.*

58 COST *which cost.*

taking coach to go to Ware, to meet a friend, it dashed me a new suit all over—a crimson satin doublet and black velvet skirts—with
65 a brewer's horse, that I was fain to go in and shift me, and kept my chamber a leash of days for the anguish of it.

Dauphine. These were dire mischances, lady.

Clerimont. I would not dwell in the city, an' 'twere so fatal to me.

Mrs. Otter. Yes, sir, but I do take advice of my doctor, to dream of
70 it as little as I can.

Dauphine. You do well, Mistress Otter.

     [*Enter Daw; Clerimont takes him aside.*]

Mrs. Otter. Will it please you to enter the house farther, gentlemen?

Dauphine. And your favor, lady; but we stay to speak with a
75 knight, Sir John Daw, who is here come. We shall follow you, lady.

Mrs. Otter. At your own time, sir. It is my cousin Sir Amorous his feast—

Dauphine. I know it, lady.

Mrs. Otter. And mine together. But it is for his honor, and
80 therefore I take no name of it, more than of the place.

Dauphine. You are a bounteous kinswoman.

Mrs. Otter. Your servant, sir. [*Exit Mrs. Otter.*]

---

63 WARE *in Hertfordshire, about 24 miles north of London; a favorite place for assignations. See the allusion to the "great bed at Ware" (V.1.57).*
 DASHED *bespattered.*

64 DOUBLET *N.*

65 SHIFT ME *change my clothes.*

66 LEASH *a set of three, originally used of hounds or hawks.*

76–77 AMOROUS HIS FEAST *Jonson called this form of the genitive (quite common between 1400 and 1750) "monstrous syntaxe" in his* English Grammar *(H & S, 8: 511).*

80 TAKE . . . PLACE *take no credit for the feast other than supplying the house for it.*

Act III Scene 3

[*Clerimont comes forward with Daw.*]
Clerimont. Why, do not you know it, Sir John Daw?
Daw. No, I am a rook if I do.

Clerimont. I'll tell you then: she's married by this time! And whereas you were put i' the head that she was gone with Sir Dauphine, I assure you Sir Dauphine has been the noblest, honest- 5 est friend to you that ever gentleman of your quality could boast of. He has discovered the whole plot, and made your mistress so acknowledging and indeed so ashamed of her injury to you, that she desires you to forgive her, and but grace her wedding with your presence today—she is to be married to a very good fortune, she 10 says, his uncle, old Morose; and she willed me in private to tell you that she shall be able to do you more favors, and with more security now than before.

Daw. Did she say so, i' faith?

Clerimont. Why, what do you think of me, Sir John? Ask Sir 15 Dauphine.

Daw. Nay, I believe you. Good Sir Dauphine, did she desire me to forgive her?

Dauphine. I assure you, Sir John, she did.

Daw. Nay, then, I do with all my heart, and I'll be jovial. 20

Clerimont. Yes, for look you, sir, this was the injury to you. La

___

2 ROOK *see I.4.70, fn. and N. to The Persons of the Play.*

4 PUT . . . HEAD *made to think.*

8 ACKNOWLEDGING *openly confessing* ("*her injury to you*").

20 JOVIAL *lit.*, "*of or pertaining to Jupiter,*" *here in an astrological sense: the state supposedly caused by the planetary influence of Jupiter. N.*

Foole intended this feast to honor her bridal day, and made you the property to invite the college ladies and promise to bring her; and then at the time she should have appeared, as his friend, to have given you the dor. Whereas now, Sir Dauphine has brought her to a feeling of it, with this kind of satisfaction, that you shall bring all the ladies to the place where she is, and be very jovial; and there she will have a dinner, which shall be in your name, and so disappoint La Foole, to make you good again and, as it were, a saver i' the main.

Daw. As I am a knight, I honor her and forgive her heartily.

Clerimont. About it then presently. Truewit is gone before to confront the coaches, and to acquaint you with so much if he meet you. Join with him, and 'tis well.

[*Enter La Foole.*]

See, here comes your antagonist, but take you no notice, but be very jovial.

La Foole. Are the ladies come, Sir John Daw, and your mistress? Sir Dauphine! You are exceeding welcome, and honest Master Clerimont. Where's my cousin? Did you see no collegiates, gentlemen? [*Exit Daw.*]

Dauphine. Collegiates! Do you not hear, Sir Amorous, how you are abused?

La Foole. How, sir!

Clerimont. Will you speak so kindly to Sir John Daw, that has done you such an affront?

La Foole. Wherein, gentlemen? Let me be a suitor to you to know, I beseech you!

23 PROPERTY *instrument, means.*

25 GIVEN . . . DOR *made you ridiculous, a laughingstock. See II.3.42 and fn.*

26 FEELING OF *sensitivity to.*

29 MAKE . . . GOOD *i.e., recover your place in society and your self-esteem.*
   SAVER . . . MAIN *N.*

31 PRESENTLY *at once.*

32 CONFRONT *meet; in this context, perhaps intercept, turn away.*
   SO MUCH *i.e., what I've just told you.*

Clerimont. Why, sir, his mistress is married today to Sir Dauphine's uncle, your cousin's neighbor, and he has diverted all the ladies and all your company thither, to frustrate your provision and stick a disgrace upon you. He was here now to have enticed us away from you too, but we told him his own, I think. 50

La Foole. Has Sir John Daw wronged me so inhumanly?

Dauphine. He has done it, Sir Amorous, most maliciously, and treacherously; but if you'll be ruled by us, you shall quit him, i'faith. 55

La Foole. Good gentlemen, I'll make one, believe it. How, I pray?

Dauphine. Marry, sir, get me your pheasants, and your godwits, and your best meat, and dish it in silver dishes of your cousin's presently, and say nothing, but clap me a clean towel about you, like a sewer, and bare-headed march afore it with a good confidence 60 —'tis but over the way, hard by—and we'll second you, where you shall set it o' the board, and bid 'em welcome to't, which shall show 'tis yours and disgrace his preparation utterly; and for your cousin, whereas she should be troubled here at home with care of making and giving welcome, she shall transfer all that labor thither and be a 65 principal guest herself, sit ranked with the college-honors, and be honored and have her health drunk as often, as bare, and as loud as the best of 'em.

La Foole. I'll go tell her presently. It shall be done, that's resolved.

[*Exit.*]

Clerimont. I thought he would not hear it out, but 'twould take 70 him.

49 PROVISION *preparations (for his feast). See below, l. 63.*
51 TOLD . . . OWN *told him his faults to his face.*
52 INHUMANLY *N.*
54 QUIT *requite, pay him back.*
56 MAKE ONE *i.e., of your group; take part.*
60 SEWER *in great households a servant of some dignity who supervises the seating and serving of guests, like a headwaiter.*
67 BARE *when toasting a lady, heads were bared.*

Dauphine. Well, there be guests and meat now; how shall we do for music?

Clerimont. The smell of the venison, going through the street, will
75 invite one noise of fiddlers or other.

Dauphine. I would it would call the trumpeters thither.

Clerimont. Faith, there is hope, they have intelligence of all feasts. There's good correspondence betwixt them and the London cooks. 'Tis twenty to one but we have 'em.

80 *Dauphine.* 'Twill be a most solemn day for my uncle, and an excellent fit of mirth for us.

Clerimont. Ay, if we can hold up the emulation betwixt Foole and Daw, and never bring them to expostulate.

Dauphine. Tut, flatter 'em both, as Truewit says, and you may
85 take their understandings in a purse-net. They'll believe themselves to be just such men as we make 'em, neither more nor less. They have nothing, not the use of their senses, but by tradition.

[*La Foole*] *enters like a sewer.*

Clerimont. See! Sir Amorous has his towel on already. Have you persuaded your cousin?

90 *La Foole.* Yes, 'tis very feasible: she'll do anything, she says, rather than the La Fooles shall be disgraced.

---

75 NOISE *any band of musicians; here, strolling fiddlers; cf. III.7.2.*

78 CORRESPONDENCE *communication; business relations.*

80 SOLEMN *distinguished by ceremony; of grave import.*

81 FIT *bout or spell; ll. 72–79 suggest a possible play on an archaic word meaning part of a song or dance.*

82 HOLD UP *maintain.*
  EMULATION *rivalry; ill will.*

83 EXPOSTULATE *protest to each other.*

85 PURSE-NET *"a bag-shaped net, whose mouth could be drawn together with cords" (OED); used especially for catching rabbits.*

87 TRADITION *the preceding sentence suggests a restricted sense: literally, what is handed over (from Latin* tradere).

Dauphine. She is a noble kinswoman. It will be such a pestling device, Sir Amorous! It will pound all your enemy's practices to powder and blow him up with his own mine, his own train.

La Foole. Nay, we'll give fire, I warrant you.   95

Clerimont. But you must carry it privately, without any noise, and take no notice by any means—

[*Re-enter Otter.*]

Otter. Gentlemen, my Princess says you shall have all her silver dishes, *festinate*; and she's gone to alter her tire a little and go with you—   100

Clerimont. And yourself too, Captain Otter?

Dauphine. By any means, sir.

Otter. Yes, sir, I do mean it; but I would entreat my cousin, Sir Amorous, and you, gentlemen, to be suitors to my Princess, that I may carry my bull and my bear, as well as my horse.   105

Clerimont. That you shall do, Captain Otter.

La Foole. My cousin will never consent, gentlemen.

Dauphine. She must consent, Sir Amorous, to reason.

La Foole. Why, she says they are no *decorum* among ladies.

Otter. But they are *decora*, and that's better, sir.   110

Clerimont. Ay, she must hear argument. Did not Pasiphae, who

---

92 PESTLING *crushing.*

94 MINE *explosive charge.*

    TRAIN *in several senses: fuse; siege artillery; retinue and supplies, civilian as well as military; trick or snare.*

99 FESTINATE *"in a hurry;" perhaps with a quibble on Italian* festino, *a small feast.*

    TIRE *attire; dress.*

109 NO DECORUM *an impropriety.*

110 DECORA *handsome, noble; Otter is pleased to play the adjectival form against the substantive.*

111 PASIPHAE *the wife of Minos and mother of Phaedra; she conceived the Minotaur from her union with a bull.*

87

was a queen, love a bull? And was not Callisto, the mother of Arcas, turned into a bear and made a star, Mistress Ursula, i' the heavens?

Otter. O God, that I could ha' said as much! I will have these
115 stories painted i' the Bear Garden, *ex Ovidii Metamorphosi.*

Dauphine. Where is your Princess, Captain? Pray be our leader.

Otter. That I shall, sir.

Clerimont. Make haste, good Sir Amorous. [*Exeunt.*]

---

112 CALLISTO *transformed first into a bear, then, on her death, into a constellation, Ursa Major, by Zeus, who loved her. Their son, Arcas, was the king from whom Arcadia supposedly derived its name.*

115 EX . . . METAMORPHOSI *N.*

Act III Scene 4

[*Morose's house.*]
[*Enter Morose, Parson, and Cutbeard with Epicoene.*]

Morose. [*To Parson.*] Sir, there's an angel for yourself, and a brace of angels for your cold. Muse not at this manage of my bounty. It is fit we should thank fortune double to nature, for any benefit she confers upon us; besides, it is your imperfection, but my solace.

5 *Parson.* I thank your worship, so is it mine now.   *The parson speaks as having a cold.*

Morose. What says he, Cutbeard?

Cutbeard. He says, *presto*, sir, whensoever your worship needs him,

---

1 ANGEL *a gold coin, then worth about 10 shillings.*

2 MANAGE *management.*

3 THANK . . . NATURE *thank "fortune," or chance, twice as much as we thank "nature," in the sense of the predictable or controllable.*

7 PRESTO *Italian; quickly, at once.*

he can be ready with the like. He got this cold with sitting up
late and singing catches with cloth-workers.

Morose. No more. I thank him.   10

Parson. God keep your worship and give you much joy with your
fair spouse. Umh, umh.   *He coughs.*

Morose. O, O, stay, Cutbeard! Let him give me five shillings of
my money back. As it is bounty to reward benefits, so is it equity to
mult injuries. I will have it. What says he?   15

Cutbeard. He cannot change it, sir.

Morose. It must be changed.

Cutbeard. [*Aside to Parson.*] Cough again.

Morose. What says he?

Cutbeard. He will cough out the rest, sir.   20

Parson. [*Coughs again.*] Umh, umh, umh.

Morose. Away, away with him, stop his mouth, away. I forgive
it— [*Exit Cutbeard with the Parson.*]

Epicoene. Fie, Master Morose, that you will use this violence to a
man of the church.   25

Morose. How!

Epicoene. It does not become your gravity or breeding—as you
pretend in court—to have offered this outrage on a waterman, or
any more boisterous creature, much less on a man of his civil coat.

Morose. You can speak then!   30

8 THE LIKE *i.e., another marriage, or another cold.*

9 CATCHES *rounds. Weavers proverbially sing as they work.*
CLOTH-WORKERS *the cloth-making industry had been established in England
largely by Protestant emigrés from the Continent, much given to psalm-singing
and hymns.*

15 MULCT *punish by a fine—here, the "injuries" caused by the Parson's coughing.*

28 PRETEND *profess to have (breeding).*
WATERMAN *boatman who rowed passengers across the Thames; notorious for
loud bickering over fares.*

29 MAN . . . COAT *man of his grave order. In the seventeenth century idiom, garb
often indicated profession.*

Epicoene. Yes, sir.

Morose. Speak out, I mean.

Epicoene. Ay, sir. Why, did you think you had married a statue?
or a motion, only? one of the French puppets with the eyes turned
35 with a wire? or some innocent out of the hospital, that would
stand with her hands thus, and a plaice mouth, and look upon you?

Morose. O immodesty! A manifest woman! What, Cutbeard!

Epicoene. Nay, never quarrel with Cutbeard, sir; it is too late now.
I confess it doth bate somewhat of the modesty I had, when I writ
40 simply maid; but I hope I shall make it a stock still competent to the
estate and dignity of your wife.

Morose. She can talk!

Epicoene. Yes, indeed, sir.

Morose. What, sirrah! None of my knaves there? [*Enter Mute.*]
45 Where is this impostor, Cutbeard? [*Mute indicates that Cutbeard has
gone.*]

Epicoene. Speak to him, fellow, speak to him. I'll have none of
this coacted, unnatural dumbness in my house, in a family where I
govern.

50   *Morose.* She is my regent already! I have married a Penthesilea, a
Semiramis, sold my liberty to a distaff!

---

34 MOTION *puppet.*
   FRENCH PUPPETS *apparently marionettes.*

35 INNOCENT *idiot, half-wit.*

36 PLAICE *puckered.*

39 IT *the behavior Morose calls "immodesty."*
   BATE *lessen, diminish, abate.*

40 STOCK *several meanings possible: the general sense of "amount" may be
   narrowed into "dowry" and may blend with "breeding" and "good family."*
   COMPETENT *proper.*

48 COACTED *enforced.*

50–51 PENTHESILEA . . . SEMIRAMIS *warrior queens: the first, of the Amazons; the
   second, of the Assyrians.*

Act III Scene 5

[Enter Truewit, as Mute goes out.]

Truewit. Where's Master Morose?

Morose. Is he come again? Lord have mercy upon me!

Truewit. I wish you all joy, Mistress Epicoene, with your grave and honorable match.

Epicoene. I return you the thanks, Master Truewit, so friendly a   5
wish deserves.

Morose. She has acquaintance too!

Truewit. God save you, sir, and give you all contentment in your fair choice here. Before, I was the bird of night to you, the owl, but now I am the messenger of peace, a dove, and bring you the glad   10
wishes of many friends to the celebration of this good hour.

Morose. What hour, sir?

Truewit. Your marriage hour, sir. I commend your resolution, that, notwithstanding all the dangers I laid afore you, in the voice of a night-crow, would yet go on, and be yourself. It shows you are   15
a man constant to your own ends, and upright to your purposes, that would not be put off with left-handed cries.

Morose. How should you arrive at the knowledge of so much?

Truewit. Why, did you ever hope, sir, committing the secrecy of it to a barber, that less than the whole town should know it? You   20
might as well ha' told it the conduit, or the bakehouse, or the in-fantry that follow the court, and with more security. Could your

9, 15 OWL, NIGHT-CROW *conventional harbingers of bad luck.*
17 LEFT-HANDED *sinister.*
21–22 CONDUIT . . . INFANTRY N.
22–23 YOUR GRAVITY *a mock-title of respect, like "your Honor."*

gravity forget so old and noted a remnant as *lippis et tonsoribus notum*?
Well, sir, forgive it yourself now, the fault, and be communicable
25 with your friends. Here will be three or four fashionable ladies from
the college to visit you presently, and their train of minions and
followers.

Morose. Bar my doors! Bar my doors! Where are all my eaters,
my mouths now? Bar up my doors, you varlets!

[Enter Servants.]

30 *Epicoene.* He is a varlet that stirs to such an office. Let 'em stand
open. I would see him that dares move his eyes toward it. Shall I
have a barricado made against my friends, to be barred of any
pleasure they can bring in to me with honorable visitation? *[Exeunt
servants.]*

35 *Morose.* O Amazonian impudence!

Truewit. Nay, faith, in this, sir, she speaks but reason, and methinks is more continent than you. Would you go to bed so presently, sir, afore noon? A man of your head and hair should owe more
to that reverend ceremony, and not mount the marriage-bed like a
40 town-bull or a mountain-goat, but stay the due season, and ascend
it then with religion and fear. Those delights are to be steeped in
the humour and silence of the night; and give the day to other open

---

23 REMNANT "*a scrap or tag of quotation*" (OED).

LIPPIS . . . NOTUM *slightly altered from Horace*, Satires *I.vii.3*: "*known to [all]
the blear-eyed [i.e., frequenters of apothecary shops] and to barbers.*"

24 FORGIVE IT YOURSELF *forgive yourself for it.*

COMMUNICABLE *communicative, ready to converse.*

28–29 EATERS . . . MOUTHS *i.e., servants.*

32 BARRICADO *rampart, fortification.*

35 IMPUDENCE *shamelessness.*

38 HEAD AND HAIR *the idiom means "judgment and character," but Truewit is
glancing ironically at Morose's appearance.*

41 RELIGION AND FEAR *i.e., as a sacrament, inspiring pious awe.*

42 HUMOUR *see III.1.11 and fn.; here the original meaning of "moisture" is stressed
by "steeped."*

pleasures and jollities of feast, of music, of revels, of discourse. We'll
have all, sir, that may make your Hymen high and happy.

Morose. O, my torment, my torment! 45

Truewit. Nay, if you endure the first half hour, sir, so tediously,
and with this irksomeness, what comfort or hope can this fair
gentlewoman make to herself hereafter, in the consideration of so
many years as are to come—

Morose. Of my affliction. Good sir, depart and let her do it alone. 50

Truewit. I have done, sir.

Morose. That cursed barber!

Truewit. Yes, faith, a cursed wretch indeed, sir.

Morose. I have married his cittern, that's common to all men.
Some plague above the plague— 55

Truewit. All Egypt's ten plagues.

Morose. —revenge me on him.

Truewit. 'Tis very well, sir. If you laid on a curse or two more,
I'll assure you he'll bear 'em. As, that he may get the pox with
seeking to cure it, sir? Or, that while he is curling another man's hair, 60
his own may drop off? Or, for burning some male bawd's lock, he
may have his brain beat out with the curling-iron?

Morose. No, let the wretch live wretched. May he get the itch and
his shop so lousy as no man dare come at him, nor he come at no
man. 65

44 HYMEN *wedding; Hymen was the god of marriage.*

48 MAKE TO *form or imagine for.*

54 CITTERN *or cithern, a musical instrument like the zither, commonly kept in
barber shops for the use of customers: hence, "common to all men."*

56 ALL . . . PLAGUES *proverbial* (Exodus *7–12*), *but suggesting a paradigm for
the dialogue that follows.*

59–61 POX . . . OFF *barbers still often practiced surgery, though after 1540 they were
formally restricted to barbering and dentistry. Their practice apparently included
treating the symptoms of "French pox," or syphilis, such as loss of hair. See
ll. 80–81, 85–86.*

63–107 *N.*

93

Act III Scene 5

Truewit. Ay, and if he would swallow all his balls for pills, let not them purge him.

Morose. Let his warming pan be ever cold.

Truewit. A perpetual frost underneath it, sir.

70 *Morose.* Let him never hope to see fire again.

Truewit. But in hell, sir.

Morose. His chairs be always empty, his scissors rust, and his combs mould in their cases.

Truewit. Very dreadful that! And may he lose the invention, sir,
75 of carving lanterns in paper.

Morose. Let there be no bawd carted that year to employ a basin of his, but let him be glad to eat his sponge for bread.

Truewit. And drink lotium to it, and much good do him.

Morose. Or, for want of bread—

80 *Truewit.* Eat ear-wax, sir. I'll help you. Or, draw his own teeth and add them to the lute string.

Morose. No, beat the old ones to powder and make bread of them.

Truewit. Yes, make meal o' the millstones.

85 *Morose.* May all the botches and burns that he has cured on others break out upon him.

Truewit. And he now forget the cure of 'em in himself, sir; or, if

66 BALLS *of soap.*

PILLS *medicinal pills, as a cathartic.*

75 LANTERNS *cheap lanterns made of oiled paper were used by barbers.*

76 BASIN *often, after bawds were sentenced, they were carted around town, and basins were beaten to attract a crowd to witness their shame.*

78 LOTIUM "*stale urine used by barbers as a 'lye' for the hair*" (OED).

80 EAR-WAX *barbers then cleaned out customers' ears.*

80–81 DRAW . . . LUTE-STRING *teeth extracted by the barber-dentist were displayed on a string in the shop, as a form of advertising.*

85 BOTCHES *boils.*

he do remember it, let him ha' scraped all his linen into lint for 't, and have not a rag left him to set up with.

Morose. Let him never set up again, but have the gout in his 90 hands forever. Now, no more, sir.

Truewit. O, that last was too high set! You might go less with him, i' faith, and be revenged enough; as, that he be never able to new-paint his pole—

Morose. Good sir, no more. I forgot myself. 95

Truewit. Or, want credit to take up with a comb-maker—

Morose. No more, sir.

Truewit. Or, having broken his glass in a former despair, fall now into a much greater, of ever getting another—

Morose. I beseech you, no more. 100

Truewit. Or, that he never be trusted with trimming of any but chimney-sweepers—

Morose. Sir—

Truewit. Or, may he cut a collier's throat with his razor, by chance-medley, and yet hang for't. 105

Morose. I will forgive him rather than hear any more. I beseech you, sir.

---

88 LINT *a soft material for dressing wounds, which was prepared by ravelling or scraping linen cloth.*

89–92 SET . . . SET *a barber sets up a business in which he sets up or "sets" hair. To curse a barber with gout in the hands is to set one's aim too high.*

92 GO LESS *wager or "set" lower stakes.*

96 WANT CREDIT . . . WITH *not be able to obtain supplies without paying for them first.*

102 CHIMNEY-SWEEPERS *with the collier (l. 104), the least desirable of customers— poor, and professionally dirty. Worse yet, a chimney-sweep's hair was an occupational fire hazard.*

104 COLLIER'S *a carrier of coal or charcoal; proverbially, dishonest.*

104–05 CHANCE-MEDLEY *legally, "casualty not purely accidental;" here, "homi-cide by misadventure" (OED).*

Act III Scene 6

[*Enter Daw with the Collegiates: Lady Haughty, Centaure, Mavis, and Trusty.*]

Daw. This way, madam.

Morose. O, the sea breaks in upon me! Another flood! An inundation! I shall be o'erwhelmed with noise. It beats already at my shores. I feel an earthquake in myself for't.

5   *Daw.* [*To Epicoene.*] Give you joy, mistress.

Morose. Has she servants too!

Daw. I have brought some ladies here to see and know you. My Lady Haughty, this my Lady Centuare, Mistress Dol   *She kisses them severally as he*
Mavis, Mistress Trusty, my Lady Haughty's woman.   *presents them.*

10   Where's your husband? Let's see him. Can he endure no noise? Let me come to him.

Morose. What *nomenclator* is this?

Truewit. Sir John Daw, sir, your wife's servant, this.

Morose. A Daw, and her servant! O, 'tis decreed, 'tis decreed

15   of me, an' she have such servants. [*He starts for the door.*]

Truewit. Nay, sir, you must kiss the ladies, you must not go away now; they come toward you to seek you out.

Haughty. I' faith, Master Morose, would you steal a marriage thus, in the midst of so many friends, and not acquaint us? Well, I'll

20   kiss you, notwithstanding the justice of my quarrel. You shall give me leave, mistress, to use a becoming familiarity with your husband.

6 SERVANTS *lovers.*

12 NOMENCLATOR *Latin, a servant who announces the names of guests.*

14–15 'TIS . . . ME *"I've been sentenced, doomed."*

19 ACQUAINT *inform.*

Epicoene. Your ladyship does me an honor in it, to let me know he is so worthy your favor; as you have done both him and me grace to visit so unprepared a pair to entertain you.

Morose. Compliment! Compliment!   25

Epicoene. But I must lay the burden of that upon my servant here.

Haughty. It shall not need, Mistress Morose; we will all bear, rather than one shall be oppressed.

Morose. I know it, and you will teach her the faculty, if she be to learn it. [*He moves as far away as he can.*]   30

Haughty. Is this the silent woman?

Centaure. Nay, she has found her tongue since she was married, Master Truewit says.

Haughty. O, Master Truewit, 'save you! What kind of creature is your bride here? She speaks, methinks!   35

Truewit. Yes, madam, believe it, she is a gentlewoman of very absolute behavior and of a good race.

Haughty. And Jack Daw told us she could not speak.

Truewit. So it was carried in plot, madam, to put her upon this old fellow, by Sir Dauphine, his nephew, and one or two more of us;   40
but she is a woman of an excellent assurance, and an extraordinary happy wit and tongue. You shall see her make rare sport with Daw ere night.

Haughty. And he brought us to laugh at her!

Truewit. That falls out often, madam, that he that thinks himself   45
the master-wit is the master-fool. I assure your ladyship, ye cannot laugh at her.

25 COMPLIMENT *ceremonious and often only formal courtesy.*
26 THAT *being unprepared.*
   SERVANT *Daw.*
29 FACULTY *ability (to bear? to lay a burden on a lover?).*
37 ABSOLUTE *perfect.*
39 CARRIED IN PLOT *managed by plotting.*
41 ASSURANCE *self-confidence.*

Act III Scene 6

Haughty. No, we'll have her to the college. An' she have wit, she shall be one of us! Shall she not, Centaure? We'll make her a
50 collegiate.

Centaure. Yes, faith, madam, and Mavis and she will set up a side.

Truewit. Believe it, madam, and Mistress Mavis, she will sustain her part.

Mavis. I'll tell you that when I have talked with her, and tried her.
55 *Haughty.* Use her very civilly, Mavis.

Mavis. So I will, madam.

[*Mavis and Epicoene move away, talking privately.*]

Morose. Blessed minute, that they would whisper thus ever.

Truewit. In the meantime, madam, would but your ladyship help to vex him a little: you know his disease, talk to him about the
60 wedding ceremonies, or call for your gloves, or—

Haughty. Let me alone. Centaure, help me. Master bridegroom, where are you?

Morose. O, it was too miraculously good to last!

Haughty. We see no ensigns of a wedding, here, no character of
65 a bridal. Where be our scarves and our gloves? I pray you, give 'em us. Let's know your bride's colors and yours at least.

Centaure. Alas, madam, he has provided none.

Morose. Had I known your ladyship's painter, I would.

Haughty. He has given it you, Centaure, i'faith. But do you hear,
70 Master Morose, a jest will not absolve you in this manner. You that have sucked the milk of the court and from thence have been brought up to the very strong meats and wine of it, been a courtier from the biggin to the night-cap, as we may say, and you to offend

51 SET . . . SIDE *become partners (in a game of cards).*

61 LET ME ALONE *i.e., I may be trusted (to vex Morose).*

64–80 ENSIGNS . . . MASQUE *N.*

68 PAINTER *i.e., the makeup artist who colored Centaure's face.*

69 GIVEN IT YOU *given you a blow (with his sarcastic remark).*

73 BIGGIN . . . NIGHT-CAP *from infancy (i.e., baby bonnet) to maturity.*

in such a high point of ceremony as this, and let your nuptials want
all marks of solemnity! How much plate have you lost today—if you   75
had but regarded your profit—what gifts, what friends, through
your mere rusticity?

Morose. Madam—

Haughty. Pardon me, sir, I must insinuate your errors to you.
No gloves? No garters? No scarves? No epithalamium? No masque?   80

Daw. Yes, madam, I'll make an epithalamium, I promised my
mistress, I have begun it already. Will your ladyship hear it?

Haughty. Ay, good Jack Daw.

Morose. Will it please your ladyship command a chamber and be
private with your friend? You shall have your choice of rooms to   85
retire to after; my whole house is yours. I know it hath been your
ladyship's errand into the city at other times, however now you
have been unhappily diverted upon me; but I shall be loath to
break any honorable custom of your ladyship's. And therefore, good
madam—   90

Epicoene. Come, you are a rude bridegroom, to entertain ladies of
honor in this fashion.

Centaure. He is a rude groom, indeed.

Truewit. By that light, you deserve to be grafted, and have your
horns reach from one side of the island to the other. [*Aside to*   95
Morose.] Do not mistake me, sir; I but speak this to give the ladies
some heart again, hot for any malice to you.

Morose. Is this your "bravo," ladies?

77 MERE RUSTICITY *utter boorishness.*

79 INSINUATE *suggest in subtle or artful ways.*

86 IT *an assignation with a lover.*

87 ERRAND *object, interest (in going).*

93 GROOM *servant; i.e., a bridegroom with the manners of a lackey.*

94 GRAFTED *made a cuckold: as in grafting, by inserting a shoot or "scion" of
alien stock into the "host" in order to produce a hybrid.*

95 HORNS *of a cuckold.*

98 BRAVO *semi-professional bully, for hire as a soldier, bodyguard, assassin, etc.*

Truewit. As God help me, if you utter such another word, I'll take
100 mistress bride in, and begin to you in a very sad cup, do you see?
Go to, know your friends and such as love you.

100 BEGIN . . . CUP *celebrate your wedding in a way most unpleasant for you. The*
phrase "begin to you" is idiomatic for "drink your health."
101 GO TO *expression of protest or impatience, like "come, come."*

Act III Scene 7

[*Enter Clerimont, with musicians.*]
Clerimont. By your leave, ladies. Do you want any music? I have
brought you variety of noises. Play, sirs, all of you. *Music of all*
sorts.
Morose. O, a plot, a plot, a plot, a plot upon me!
This day I shall be their anvil to work on, they will grate me
5 asunder. 'Tis worse than the noise of a saw.
Clerimont. No, they are hair, rosin, and guts. I can give you the
receipt.
Truewit. Peace, boys.
Clerimont. Play, I say.
10 *Truewit.* Peace, rascals. [*To Morose.*] You see who's your friend
now, sir? Take courage, put on a martyr's resolution. Mock down all
their attemptings with patience. 'Tis but a day, and I would suffer

2 NOISES *groups of musicians, as in III.3.75, but suggesting the "several noises"*
of affliction in II.6.35.

4 GRATE *grind.*

6 HAIR . . . GUTS *Clerimont solemnly corrects Morose's figurative agonizing over*
the noise by referring to the physical materials in violins which cause the music—
sheep-gut (the strings), horsehair (the bow), rosin (to roughen the hair of the bow).

7 RECEIPT *formula, recipe.*

heroically. Should an ass exceed me in fortitude? No. You betray your infirmity with your hanging dull ears, and make them insult. Bear up bravely and constantly. *La Foole passes over, sewing the meat,* 15 *[with servants. Mistress Otter follows.]* Look you here, sir, what honor is done you unexpected by your nephew; a wedding dinner come, and a knight-sewer before it, for the more reputation: and fine Mistress Otter, your neighbor, in the rump or tail of it.

Morose. Is that Gorgon, that Medusa come? Hide me, hide me. 20

Truewit. I warrant you, sir, she will not transform you. Look upon her with a good courage. Pray you entertain her and conduct your guests in. No? Mistress bride, will you entreat in the ladies? Your bridegroom is so shamefaced here—

Epicoene. Will it please your ladyship, madam? 25

Haughty. With the benefit of your company, mistress.

Epicoene. Servant, pray you perform your duties.

Daw. And glad to be commanded, mistress.

Centaure. How like you her wit, Mavis?

Mavis. Very prettily, absolutely well. 30

Mrs. Otter. 'Tis my place.

Mavis. You shall pardon me, Mistress Otter.

Mrs. Otter. Why, I am a collegiate.

Mavis. But not in ordinary.

Mrs. Otter. But I am. 35

13 ASS . . . FORTITUDE *Truewit ironically uses the donkey, an old type of stupidity, as his instance of fortitude, partly to allude to Morose's sensitive hearing ("hanging dull ears," l. 14).*

14 INSULT *exult, brag.*

15 CONSTANTLY *steadfastly.*
   SEWING *directing the serving of; see III.3.60 and fn.*

21 TRANSFORM *in myth, looking on a Gorgon (l. 20) turned one into stone. See II.4.11–14.*

31 'TIS . . . PLACE *i.e., to pass on Epicoene's wit; "place" means rank and its privileges, and also subject or topic (Latin locus).*

34 IN ORDINARY *see II.3.89 and fn.*

Mavis. We'll dispute that within. [*Exeunt Ladies with Daw.*]

Clerimont. Would this had lasted a little longer.

[*Enter Otter.*]

Truewit. And that they had sent for the heralds. Captain Otter, what news?

40 *Otter.* I have brought my bull, bear, and horse in private, and yonder are the trumpeters without, and the drum, gentlemen.

Morose. O, O, O! *The Drum and Trumpets sound.*

Otter. And we will have a rouse in each of 'em anon, for bold Britons, i'faith.

45 *Morose.* O, O, O!

All. Follow, follow, follow! [*Morose runs off, with the others following.*]

38 HERALDS *i.e., to settle the question of "place" or precedence in the preceding dialogue, and for the sake of the (loud) fanfare accompanying heraldic ceremony.*

43 ROUSE *full draught of liquor.*

Act IV Scene 1

[*Morose's house.*]
[*Enter Truewit and Clerimont.*]

Truewit. Was there ever poor bridegroom so tormented, or man, indeed?

Clerimont. I have not read of the like in the chronicles of the land.

Truewit. Sure, he cannot but go to a place of rest after all this purgatory.   5

Clerimont. He may presume it, I think.

Truewit. The spitting, the coughing, the laughter, the neesing, the farting, dancing, noise of the music, and her masculine and loud commanding, and urging the whole family, makes him think he has married a Fury.   10

Clerimont. And she carries it up bravely.

Truewit. Ay, she takes any occasion to speak: that's the height on't.

Clerimont. And how soberly Dauphine labors to satisfy him that it was none of his plot!   15

Truewit. And has almost brought him to the faith, i' the article.

4 PLACE OF REST *Paradise.*

7 NEESING *sneezing.*

9 URGING . . . FAMILY *provoking all the servants.*

12–13 HEIGHT ON'T *high point (of Morose's discomfort and their enjoyment).*

Act IV Scene I

Here he comes. [*Enter Dauphine.*] Where is he now? What's become
of him, Dauphine?

    Dauphine. O, hold me up a little, I shall go away i' the jest else. He
20 has got on his whole nest of night-caps, and locked himself up i'
the top of the house, as high as ever he can climb from the noise.
I peeped in at a cranny and saw him sitting over a cross-beam o' the
roof, like him o' the saddler's horse in Fleet Street, upright; and he
will sleep there.

25 *Clerimont.* But where are your collegiates?

    Dauphine. Withdrawn with the bride in private.

    Truewit. O, they are instructing her i' the college grammar. If she
have grace with them, she knows all their secrets instantly.

    Clerimont. Methinks the Lady Haughty looks well today, for all
30 my dispraise of her i' the morning. I think I shall come about to
thee again, Truewit.

    Truewit. Believe it, I told you right. Women ought to repair the
losses time and years have made i' their features, with dressings. And
an intelligent woman, if she know by herself the least defect, will
35 be most curious to hide it, and it becomes her. If she be short, let
her sit much, lest when she stands she be thought to sit. If she have
an ill foot, let her wear her gown the longer and her shoe the
thinner. If a fat hand and scald nails, let her carve the less, and act in

19 GO . . . JEST *die laughing.*

20 NEST *set of similar objects of diminishing sizes.*

23 SADDLER'S HORSE *N.*

28 HAVE . . . THEM *be in their good graces.*

30–31 COME . . . THEE *come around to your opinion; see I.1.77–113 for the earlier
difference of opinion.*

32–113 *N.*

34 BY *about, in reference to.*

35 CURIOUS *careful.*

38 SCALD (*trans.* Ovid's scaber) *scabrous, rough; from skin disease called "scall."*
CARVE *gesture ("act") affectedly at table, presumably as flirtation; for other
examples, see H & S.*

104

gloves. If a sour breath, let her never discourse fasting, and always talk
at her distance. If she have black and rugged teeth, let her offer the   40
less at laughter, especially if she laugh wide and open.

Clerimont. O, you shall have some women, when they laugh, you
would think they brayed, it is so rude and—

Truewit. Ay, and others, that will stalk i' their gait like an ostrich,
and take huge strides. I cannot endure such a sight. I love measure   45
i' the feet and number i' the voice: they are gentlenesses that oft-
times draw no less than the face.

Dauphine. How cam'st thou to study these creatures so exactly?
I would thou would'st make me a proficient.

Truewit. Yes, but you must leave to live i' your chamber, then,   50
a month together, upon *Amadis de Gaul* or *Don Quixote*, as you are
wont, and come abroad where the matter is frequent, to court, to
tiltings, public shows and feasts, to plays, and church sometimes;
thither they come to show their new tires too, to see and to be seen.
In these places a man shall find whom to love, whom to play with,   55
whom to touch once, whom to hold ever. The variety arrests his
judgment. A wench to please a man comes not down dropping from

44 ostrich] Estrich F.

---

39 DISCOURSE FASTING *talk while fasting (because breath is particularly sour on an
  empty stomach).*
40 RUGGED *rough, uneven.*
45–46 MEASURE . . . FEET *grace and proportion in moving, suggesting the rhythmical
  patterns of dance.*
  NUMBER *musical cadence, as in song or verse.*
46 GENTLENESSES *"elegancies" (OED, citing this passage); charms, graces.*
50 LEAVE TO LIVE *stop living (infinitive used for gerund).*
51 AMADIS . . . QUIXOTE *N.*
52 MATTER IS FREQUENT *subject of study is plentiful.*
53 TILTINGS *joustings, tournaments, often in semi-dramatic form like a pageant or
  masque.*
56 ARRESTS *catches, engages.*

the ceiling, as he lies on his back droning a tobacco pipe. He must go where she is.

60   *Dauphine.* Yes, and be never the near.

    Truewit. Out, heretic. That diffidence makes thee worthy it should be so.

    Clerimont. He says true to you, Dauphine.

    Dauphine. Why?

65   *Truewit.* A man should not doubt to overcome any woman. Think he can vanquish 'em, and he shall: for though they deny, their desire is to be tempted. Penelope herself cannot hold out long. Ostend, you saw, was taken at last. You must persèver and hold to your purpose. They would solicit us, but that they are afraid. How-

70 soever, they wish in their hearts we should solicit them. Praise 'em, flatter 'em, you shall never want eloquence or trust; even the chastest delight to feel themselves that way rubbed. With praises you must mix kisses too. If they take them, they'll take more. Though they strive, they would be overcome.

75   *Clerimont.* O, but a man must beware of force.

68 persèver] persevere F₃.

---

58 DRONING *as if playing the "drone," or base pipe, of a bagpipe which emits only one continuous tone.*

60 NEAR *nerarer (the old comparative of "nigh").*

61–62 THAT . . . SO *your lack of confidence makes you deserve to get no closer to women.*

65 DOUBT *mistrust his ability.*

66 DENY *say "no".*

68 OSTEND *Dutch-held port in Flanders, besieged by the Spanish from July 1601 to Sept. 1604.*

70–71 PRAISE . . . TRUST *i.e., flatter women, and they always think you eloquent and trustworthy.*

72 RUBBED *annoyed; pressed or touched; perhaps, as in bowling, blocked or diverted.*

74 STRIVE *struggle, resist.*
    WOULD BE *want to be.*

Truewit. It is to them an acceptable violence, and has oft-times the place of the greatest courtesy. She that might have been forced, and you let her go free without touching, though she then seem to thank you, will ever hate you after; and glad i' the face, is assuredly sad at the heart.   80

Clerimont. But all women are not to be taken all ways.

Truewit. 'Tis true. No more than all birds or all fishes. If you appear learned to an ignorant wench, or jocund to a sad, or witty to a foolish, why, she presently begins to mistrust herself. You must approach them i' their own height, their own line; for the contrary   85
makes many that fear to commit themselves to noble and worthy fellows, run into the embraces of a rascal. If she love wit, give verses, though you borrow 'em of a friend, or buy 'em, to have good. If valor, talk of your sword, and be frequent in the mention of quarrels, though you be staunch in fighting. If activity, be seen o'   90
your Barbary often, or leaping over stools, for the credit of your back. If she love good clothes or dressing, have your learned council about you every morning, your French tailor, barber, linener, etc. Let your powder, your glass, and your comb be your dearest acquaintance. Take more care for the ornament of your head than the safety, and   95
wish the commonwealth rather troubled than a hair about you. That will take her. Then if she be covetous and craving, do you promise anything, and perform sparingly; so shall you keep her in appetite still. Seem as you would give, but be like a barren field that yields

81 all ways] alwaies F, Q. See N.

---

84 MISTRUST HERSELF *be doubtful of her own power (to attract a man).*

85 I' ... LINE *on their own terms. "Height" and "line" may be geographical metaphors for latitude and longitude. See V.1.22 fn.*

90 STAUNCH *"restrained" (Beaurline); "really brave, and so not inclined to boast" (H & S).*

   ACTIVITY *physical exercise, sports; often in a sexual sense.*

91 BARBARY *horse, of stock native to Barbary.*

   FOR ... BACK *to recommend your strength (implying sexual prowess).*

100 little, or unlucky dice to foolish and hoping gamesters. Let your
gifts be slight and dainty rather than precious. Let cunning be above
cost. Give cherries at time of year, or apricots; and say they were
sent you out o' the country, though you bought 'em in Cheapside.
Admire her tires, like her in all fashions, compare her in every
105 habit to some deity, invent excellent dreams to flatter her, and riddles; or, if she be a great one, perform always the second parts to her:
like what she likes, praise whom she praises, and fail not to make
the household and servants yours, yea, the whole family, and
salute 'em by their names—'tis but light cost if you can purchase
110 'em so—and make her physician your pensioner, and her chief
woman. Nor will it be out of your gain to make love to her too, so
she follow, not usher, her lady's pleasure. All blabbing is taken
away when she comes to be a part of the crime.

    Dauphine. On what courtly lap hast thou late slept, to come forth
115 so sudden and absolute a courtling?

    Truewit. Good faith, I should rather question you, that are so
hark'ning after these mysteries. I begin to suspect your diligence,
Dauphine. Speak, art thou in love in earnest?

    Dauphine. Yes, by my troth, am I! 'Twere ill dissembling before
120 thee.

101–02 LET . . . COST *i.e., let your skill be greater than your expense.*

102 AT . . . YEAR *in season.*

103 CHEAPSIDE *the chief market place of London.*

106 GREAT ONE *lady of rank or renown.*

    PERFORM . . . SECOND PARTS *a theatrical phrase (Latin, agere secundae partes): act a subordinate role, play second fiddle.*

108 YOURS *i.e., loyal to you.*

110 PENSIONER *hireling.*

110–11 CHIEF WOMAN *most influential or favored attendant; personal maid.*

    OUT . . . GAIN *beyond or contrary to your interests.*

112 USHER *go before (as an escort).*

117 MYSTERIES *highly technical skills; esoteric doctrine.*

    DILIGENCE *careful attention (to "these mysteries").*

Truewit. With which of 'em, I pray thee?

Dauphine. With all the collegiates.

Clerimont. Out on thee! We'll keep you at home, believe it, i' the stable, an' you be such a stallion.

Truewit. No. I like him well. Men should love wisely, and all 125 women: some one for the face, and let her please the eye; another for the skin, and let her please the touch; a third for the voice, and let her please the ear; and where the objects mix, let the senses so too. Thou would'st think it strange if I should make 'em all in love with thee afore night! 130

Dauphine. I would say thou had'st the best philtre i' the world, and could'st do more than Madam Medea or Doctor Foreman.

Truewit. If I do not, let me play the mountebank for my meat while I live, and the bawd for my drink.

Dauphine. So be it, I say. 135

---

123 OUT ON THEE *interjection expressing reproach or indignation.*

125 LIKE . . . WELL *approve of him (i.e., for loving all the collegiates).*

131 PHILTRE *a potion or drug supposedly capable of exciting sexual love.*

132 MEDEA *celebrated for her skill in mixing magic philtres, one of which she used to restore Jason's old father, Aeson, to youthful vigor.*
DOCTOR FOREMAN *a famous astrologer and quack (1552–1611), reputedly able to supply love-philtres.*

Act IV Scene 2

[*Enter Otter, carrying his cups, with Daw and La Foole.*]

Otter. O lord, gentlemen, how my knights and I have missed you here!

Clerimont. Why, Captain, what service, what service?

Act IV Scene 2

Otter. To see me bring up my bull, bear, and horse to fight.
5 *Daw.* Yes, faith, the Captain says we shall be his dogs to bait 'em.
Dauphine. A good employment.
Truewit. Come on, let's see a course then.
La Foole. I am afraid my cousin will be offended if she come.
Otter. Be afraid of nothing. Gentlemen, I have placed the drum
10 and the trumpets and one to give 'em the sign when you are ready.
[*Handing around his cups.*] Here's my bull for myself, and my bear
for Sir John Daw, and my horse for Sir Amorous. Now, set your foot
to mine, and yours to his, and—
La Foole. Pray God my cousin come not.
15 *Otter.* Saint George and Saint Andrew, fear no cousins. Come,
sound, sound! *Et rauco strepuerunt cornua cantu.* [*Drum and trumpets
sound. They drink.*]
Truewit. Well said, Captain, i' faith; well fought at the bull.
Clerimont. Well held at the bear.
20 *Truewit.* Low, low, Captain!
Dauphine. O, the horse has kicked off his dog already.
La Foole. I cannot drink it, as I am a knight.
Truewit. Gods so! Off with his spurs, somebody.

4–5 BULL . . . BAIT *N.*
  7 COURSE *each attack on the bear by dogs in bearbaiting was called a course. Here,
   a round of drinks. See l. 134.*
10 ONE *i.e., someone.*
12–13 SET . . . MINE *snatch of a popular Elizabethan song, "Uptails All": "set your
   foot to my foot, and uptails all." Otter and the other drinkers touch their cups
   together and drain them.*
15 SAINT GEORGE AND SAINT ANDREW *patron saints of England and Scotland,
   newly joined in 1603 when James VI of Scotland became James I of England.*
16 ET . . . CANTU *"And with hoarse note his trumpets blared" (when Turnus is
   mustering his forces). Virgil, Aeneid, viii.2.*
18 WELL SAID *well done (i.e., "assayed"? OED Say, vb.2).*
20 LOW *not "high and fair" like Daw (l. 27).*
23 GODS SO *see II.4.89 and fn.*
  OFF . . . SPURS *punishment for cowardly knight.*

110

La Foole. It goes against my conscience. My cousin will be angry with it. 25

Daw. I ha' done mine.

Truewit. You fought high and fair, Sir John.

Clerimont. At the head.

Dauphine. Like an excellent bear-dog.

Clerimont. [*Aside to Daw.*] You take no notice of the business, I 30
hope.

Daw. [*Aside to Clerimont.*] Not a word, sir; you see we are jovial.

Otter. Sir Amorous, you must not equivocate. It must be pulled down, for all my cousin.

Clerimont. [*Aside to La Foole.*] 'Sfoot, if you take not your drink, 35
they'll think you are discontented with something; you'll betray all if you take the least notice.

La Foole. [*Aside to Clerimont.*] Not I, I'll both drink and talk then.

Otter. You must pull the horse on his knees, Sir Amorous; fear no cousins. *Jacta est alea.* 40

Truewit. [*Aside to Clerimont.*] O, now he's in his vein, and bold. The least hint given him of his wife now will make him rail desperately.

Clerimont. [*Aside to Truewit.*] Speak to him of her.

Truewit. [*Aside to Clerimont.*] Do you, and I'll fetch her to the 45
hearing of it. [*Exit.*]

Dauphine. Captain He-Otter, your She-Otter is coming, your wife.

Otter. Wife! Buz! *Titivilitium!* There's no such thing in nature.

33–34 IT . . . DOWN *1. the liquor must be drunk 2. the animal (continuing the analogy to bearbaiting) must be brought to the ground. See l. 39.*

40 JACTA EST ALEA " *The die is cast*" (*phrase made famous by Caesar when he moved his army across the Rubicon and thus declared war on the Republic*).

41 IN . . . VEIN *the "humour" for which he is known (III.1.11–13), described by Truewit in II.6.48–53.*

43 DESPERATELY *recklessly.*

50 I confess, gentlemen, I have a cook, a laundress, a house-drudge, that serves my necessary turns, and goes under that title. But he's an ass that will be so uxurious to tie his affections to one circle. Come, the name dulls appetite. Here, replenish again; another bout. Wives are nasty, sluttish animals. [*Fills the cups again.*]

55 *Dauphine.* O, Captain.

Otter. As ever the earth bare, *tribus verbis.* Where's Master Truewit?

Daw. He's slipped aside, sir.

Clerimont. But you must drink and be jovial.

60 *Daw.* Yes, give it me.

La Foole. And me, too.

Daw. Let's be jovial.

La Foole. As jovial as you will.

Otter. Agreed. Now you shall ha' the bear, cousin, and Sir John

65 Daw the horse, and I'll ha' the bull still. Sound, Tritons o' the Thames. *Nunc est bibendum, nunc pede libero*—

Morose. Villains, murderers, sons of the earth, and traitors, what do you there?

Clerimont. O, now the trumpets have waked him we

70 shall have his company.

Otter. A wife is a scurvy clogdogdo, an unlucky thing, a very

Morose speaks from above: the trumpets sounding.

---

49 BUZ *an exclamation of impatience or contempt. See* Hamlet, *II.2.412.*

TITIVILITIUM (*Latin; coined by Pla·us in* Casina, *347*) "*A vile thing of no value. A rotten threede.*" T. Cooper, Thesaurus (*1584*).

52 ASS . . . CIRCLE *an ass tied to a rotary mill.*

56 TRIBUS VERBIS *in three words; i.e., to put it bluntly.*

65 TRITONS *sea deities who, like the original Triton, ride sea horses and blow "wreathed horns" made of conch shells.*

66 NUNC . . . LIBERO "*now is the time for drinking* [*and stamping on the ground*] *with unfettered foot.*" Horace, Odes, *I.xxxvii. N.*

67 SONS . . . EARTH "*terrae filius*" *in late Latin means lowborn or bastard; roughly, "son of a bitch."*

71 CLOGDOGDO *N.*

foresaid bear-whelp, without any good fashion or breeding:
mala bestia.   *His wife is*
    Dauphine. Why did you marry one then, Captain? *brought out to*
    Otter. A pox—I married with six thousand pound, *Truewit.]* 75
I. I was in love with that. I ha' not kissed my Fury these forty
weeks.
    Clerimont. The more to blame you, Captain.
               [*Truewit restrains Mrs. Otter.*]
    Truewit. Nay, Mistress Otter, hear him a little first.
    Otter. She has a breath worse than my grandmother's, *profecto.* 80
    Mrs. Otter. O treacherous liar! Kiss me, sweet Master Truewit,
and prove him a slandering knave.
    Truewit. I'll rather believe you, lady.
    Otter. And she has a peruke that's like a pound of hemp made
up in shoe-threads. 85
    Mrs. Otter. O viper, mandrake!
    Otter. A most vile face! And yet she spends me forty pound a year
in mercury and hogs' bones. All her teeth were made i' the Blackfriars, both her eyebrows i' the Strand, and her hair in Silver Street.
Every part o' the town owns a piece of her. 90
    Mrs. Otter. I cannot hold.
    Otter. She takes herself asunder still when she goes to bed, into
some twenty boxes, and about next day noon is put together again,

---

71–72 VERY FORESAID 1. *absolutely decreed or predictable* 2. *possibly "forsaid",
forbidden.*

73 MALA BESTIA *dangerous animal.* N.

80 PROFECTO *certainly.*

85 SHOE-THREADS *shoe laces.*

86 MANDRAKE *a corruption of mandragora, a plant whose forked root, somewhat
like that of a human figure, and narcotic effect, made it a useful term of abuse.*

88 MERCURY . . . BONES *used in making cosmetics.*

88–90 TEETH . . . HER N.

like a great German clock; and so comes forth and rings a tedious
95 'larum to the whole house, and then is quiet again for an hour,
but for her quarters. Ha' you done me right, gentlemen?

   Mrs. Otter. No, sir, I'll do you right with my   *She falls upon*
quarters, with my quarters.   *him and beats*
   him.

   Otter. O, hold, good Princess.   [*Musicians*
100   *Truewit.* Sound, sound!   *enter with drums*
     and trumpets
   Clerimont. A battle, a battle!   *sounding.*]

   Mrs. Otter. You notorious stinkardly bearward, does my breath
smell?

   Otter. Under correction, dear Princess. Look to my bear and my
105 horse, gentlemen.

   Mrs. Otter. Do I want teeth and eyebrows, thou bulldog?

   Truewit. Sound, sound still!   [*Drums and*
   trumpets again.]
   Otter. No, I protest, under correction—

   Mrs. Otter. Ay, now you are under correction, you protest; but
110 you did not protest before correction, sir. Thou Judas, to offer to
betray thy Princess! I'll make thee an example—

   Morose. I will have no such examples in my house,   *Morose descends*
Lady Otter.   *with a long*
   sword.

   Mrs. Otter. Ah— [*She screams.*]

115   *Morose.* Mrs. Mary Ambree, your examples are dangerous.
Rogues, hellhounds, Stentors, out of my doors, you sons of noise

---

95 'LARUM *alarm: clock's chimes; call to arms, or battle-cry.*

96–98 QUARTERS . . . QUARTERS *N.*

96 DONE ME RIGHT *drunk with or to me.*

97–98 SD SHE . . . HIM *N.*

102 BEARWARD *keeper of a bear who leads it about for public exhibition.*

104 UNDER CORRECTION *see III.1.9 fn.*

115 MARY AMBREE *an Amazonian heroine of a ballad who according to legend took part in the attempt to recapture Ghent in 1584.*

116 STENTORS *Stentor, the Greek herald at Troy, had an "iron voice" as loud as the shout of fifty men.*

and tumult, begot on an ill May day, or when the
galley-foist is afloat to Westminster! A trumpeter
could not be conceived but then!

Dauphine. What ails you, sir?

[*She runs off,
followed by
Daw and La
Foole, as he
chases the
musicians away.*]   120

Morose. They have rent my roof, walls, and all my windores
asunder with their brazen throats. [*Exit.*]

Truewit. Best follow him, Dauphine.

Dauphine. So I will. [*Exit.*]

Clerimont. Where's Daw and La Foole?   125

Otter. They are both run away, sir. Good gentlemen, help to pacify
my Princess, and speak to the great ladies for me. Now must I go lie
with the bears this fortnight, and keep out o' the way till my peace
be made, for this scandal she has taken. Did you not see my bull-
head, gentlemen?   130

Clerimont. Is 't not on, Captain?

Truewit. No, but he may make a new one, by that is on.

Otter. O, here 'tis. An' you come over, gentlemen, and ask for
Tom Otter, we'll go down to Ratcliff, and have a course i' faith, for
all these disasters. There's *bona spes* left.   135

Truewit. Away, Captain, get off while you are well. [*Exit Otter.*]

Clerimont. I am glad we are rid of him.

Truewit. You had never been, unless we had put his wife upon
him. His humour is as tedious at last, as it was ridiculous at first.

[*Exeunt.*]

117 ILL MAY DAY *N.*

118 GALLEY-FOIST *the state barge which brought the Lord Mayor to Westminster
to be sworn in on Lord Mayor's day, an especially noisy affair, with drumming,
piping, trumpeting, and firing of cannons.*

129 SCANDAL *offence.*

131 ON *i.e., on Otter's shoulders, perhaps alluding to the bumps Otter's wife made on
his head, perhaps to horns, hinting that Otter is a cuckold.*

132 BY THAT *by copying the one that* . . .

134 RATCLIFF *on the Thames, below London; a popular rendezvous for activities
likely to come "under correction" within the city limits.*

135 BONA SPES *good hope.*

Act IV Scene 3

[*Enter Haughty, Mrs. Otter, Mavis, Daw, La Foole, Centaure, and Epicoene.*]

Haughty. We wondered why you shrieked so, Mrs. Otter.

Mrs. Otter. O God, madam, he came down with a huge long naked weapon in both his hands, and looked so dreadfully! Sure, he's beside himself.

5 *Mavis.* Why, what made you there, Mistress Otter?

Mrs. Otter. Alas, Mistress Mavis, I was chastising my subject, and thought nothing of him.

Daw. [*To Epicoene.*] Faith, mistress, you must do so too. Learn to chastise. Mistress Otter corrects her husband so, he dares not speak

10 but under correction.

La Foole. And with his hat off to her; 'twould do you good to see.

Haughty. In sadness, 'tis good and mature counsel; practice it, Morose. I'll call you Morose still now, as I call Centaure and

15 Mavis; we four will be all one.

Centaure. And you'll come to the college and live with us?

Haughty. Make him give milk and honey.

Mavis. Look how you manage him at first, you shall have him ever after.

5 WHAT . . . THERE *what were you doing there.*

13 IN SADNESS *seriously; in earnest.*

14 CALL . . . MOROSE *i.e., by her husband's name, a modish form of familiar address, but here suggesting usurpation or reversal of roles; see N. on Otter's beating, IV.2.103–05, and Introd., pp. 15–17.*

STILL *always.*

17 MILK . . . HONEY *as in the Promised Land (Exodus 3: 8).*

Centaure. Let him allow you your coach and four horses, your   20
woman, your chambermaid, your page, your gentleman-usher,
your French cook, and four grooms.

Haughty. And go with us to Bedlam, to the china-houses, and to
the Exchange.

Centaure. It will open the gate to your fame.   25

Haughty. Here's Centaure has immortalized herself with taming
of her wild male.

Mavis. Ay, she has done the miracle of the kingdom.

         [*Clerimont and Truewit enter and observe.*]

Epicoene. But, ladies, do you count it lawful to have such plurality
of servants, and do 'em all graces?   30

Haughty. Why not? Why should women deny their favors to
men? Are they the poorer, or the worse?

Daw. Is the Thames the less for the dyers' water, mistress?

La Foole. Or a torch for lighting many torches?

Truewit. [*Aside.*] Well said, La Foole; what a new one he has got!   35

Centaure. They are empty losses women fear in this kind.

Haughty. Besides, ladies should be mindful of the approach of
age, and let no time want his due use. The best of our days pass first.

Mavis. We are rivers that cannot be called back, madam: she that

23 BEDLAM *hospital of St. Mary of Bethlehem, first mentioned as an asylum for
lunatics in 1402, and later (until the 1770s) visited, for a fee, as entertainment.*

23–24 CHINA-HOUSES . . . EXCHANGE *see I.3.36–37 and fn.; also I.4.27 and fn.*

28 SD *N.*

29 PLURALITY *perhaps a play on ecclesiastical plurality: the simultaneous holding
of more than one benefice or living by one person.*

30 DO . . . GRACES *do honor to them—here, give her favors to them.*

33–34 THAMES . . . TORCHES *N.*

33 DYERS' WATER *discolored waste, discharge into the river.*

34 TORCH . . . TORCHES *"As the Candle that is carried in a Lanthorne, shall light
many Candles, and yet loose no part of his own light." Robert Cawdrey, A
Treasurie or Store-house of Similes (1600), p. 478.*

35 NEW ONE *i.e., novel or original figure; spoken ironically: a cliché.*

40 now excludes her lovers may live to lie a forsaken beldam in a frozen
bed.

Centaure. 'Tis true, Mavis; and who will wait on us to coach
then, or write, or tell us the news then? make anagrams of our
names, and invite us to the cockpit, and kiss our hands all the
45 play-time, and draw their weapons for our honors?

Haughty. Not one.

Daw. Nay, my mistress is not altogether unintelligent of these
things; here be in presence have tasted of her favors.

Clerimont. [*Aside.*] What a neighing hobby-horse is this!

50 *Epicoene.* But not with intent to boast 'em again, servant. And
have you those excellent receipts, madam, to keep yourselves from
bearing of children?

Haughty. O, yes, Morose. How should we maintain our youth
and beauty else? Many births of a woman make her old, as many
55 crops make the earth barren.

40 BELDAM *loathsome old woman.*

42 WAIT ON *escort.*

43–44 MAKE . . . NAMES *transpose the letters to form a flattering word, pet name, etc.*

44 COCKPIT *though the reference is probably general, collegiate pretension may
suggest the Cockpit-in-Court at Whitehall, which also served as a small private
theater.*

49 HOBBY-HORSE *foolish fellow.* N.

Act IV Scene 4

[*Enter Morose and Dauphine.*]

Morose. O my cursed angel, that instructed me to this fate!

Dauphine. Why, sir?

1 INSTRUCTED *directed.*

118

Morose. That I should be seduced by so foolish a devil as a barber will make!

Dauphine. I would I had been worthy, sir, to have partaken your counsel; you should never have trusted it to such a minister. 5

Morose. Would I could redeem it with the loss of an eye, nephew, a hand, or any other member.

Dauphine. Marry, God forbid, sir, that you should geld yourself to anger your wife. 10

Morose. So it would rid me of her! And that I did supererogatory penance, in a belfry, at Westminster Hall, i' the cockpit, at the fall of a stag, the Tower Wharf—what place is there else?—London Bridge, Paris Garden, Billingsgate, when the noises are at their height and loudest. Nay, I would sit out a play that were nothing but fights 15 at sea, drum, trumpet, and target!

Dauphine. I hope there shall be no such need, sir. Take patience, good uncle. This is but a day, and 'tis well worn too now.

Morose. O, 'twill be so forever, nephew, I foresee it, forever. Strife and tumult are the dowry that comes with a wife. 20

Truewit. I told you so, sir, and you would not believe me.

Morose. Alas, do not rub those wounds, Master Truewit, to blood again; 'twas my negligence. Add not affliction to affliction. I have perceived the effect of it, too late, in Madame Otter.

Epicoene. [Approaching Morose.] How do you, sir? 25

Morose. Did you ever hear a more unnecessary question? As if she did not see! Why, I do as you see, Empress, Empress.

Epicoene. You are not well, sir! You look very ill! Something has distempered you.

11 THAT I DID *i.e.,* "*I would do.*"

12–14 BELFRY . . . BILLINGSGATE *N.*

16 TARGET *shield,* "*buckler;*" *the traditional sword and buckler, considered old-fashioned compared to the rapier, were no doubt noisier.*

29 DISTEMPERED *upset; lit.,* "*out of temper,*" *i.e., disorder of the balanced (or* "*tempered*") *mixture of the four bodily humours thought to determine emotional, physical, and mental equilibrium.*

30   *Morose.* O horrible, monstrous impertinencies! Would not one of these have served? Do you think, sir? Would not one of these have served?

   Truewit. Yes, sir, but these are but notes of female kindness, sir; certain tokens that she has a voice, sir.

35   *Morose.* O, is't so? Come, an't be no otherwise—what say you?

   Epicoene. How do you feel yourself, sir?

   Morose. Again, that!

   Truewit. Nay, look you, sir; you would be friends with your wife upon unconscionable terms, her silence—

40   *Epicoene.* They say you are run mad, sir.

   Morose. Not for love, I assure you, of you, do you see?

   Epicoene. O lord, gentlemen! Lay hold on him, for God's sake. What shall I do? Who's his physician, can you tell, that knows the state of his body best, that I might send for him? Good sir, speak.

45   I'll send for one of my doctors, else.

   Morose. What, to poison me, that I might die intestate, and leave you possessed of all?

   Epicoene. Lord, how idly he talks, and how his eyes sparkle! He looks green about the temples! Do you see what blue spots he has?

50   *Clerimont.* Ay, it's melancholy.

   Epicoene. Gentlemen, for heaven's sake, counsel me. Ladies! Servant, you have read Pliny and Paracelsus: ne'er a word now to

33 KINDNESS *a quibble: gentle nature; natural inclination.*

39 UNCONSCIONABLE *unreasonable; excessive.*

46 INTESTATE *N.*

48 IDLY *incoherently, deliriously.*

50 MELANCHOLY *N.*

52 PLINY *the Elder* (A.D. *23–79*), *author of the* Historia Naturalis, *an encyclopedic account of natural phenomena as known and understood in classical antiquity. N.* PARACELSUS *adopted name of Philippus Aureolus Theophrastus Bombastus von Hohenheim* (*1493–1541*), *controversial German–Swiss physician, surgeon, and alchemist, violent opponent of the traditional authorities, classical and scholastic. N.*

comfort a poor gentlewoman? Ay me! What fortune had I to marry a distracted man?

Daw. I'll tell you, mistress— 55

Truewit. [*Aside to Clerimont.*] How rarely she holds it up!

Morose. What mean you, gentlemen?

Epicoene. What will you tell me, servant?

Daw. The disease in Greek is called μανία, in Latin, *Insania, Furor, vel Ecstasis melancholica,* that is, *Egressio,* when a man *ex* 60 *melancholico evadit fanaticus.*

Morose. Shall I have a lecture read upon me alive?

Daw. But he may be but *Phreneticus* yet, mistress, and *Phrenetis* is only *delirium* or so—

Epicoene. Ay, that is for the disease, servant; but what is this to the 65 cure? We are sure enough of the disease.

Morose. Let me go.

Truewit, Why, we'll entreat her to hold her peace, sir.

Morose. O, no. Labor not to stop her. She is like a conduit-pipe that will gush out with more force when she opens again. 70

Haughty. I'll tell you, Morose, you must talk divinity to him altogether, or moral philosophy.

La Foole. Ay, and there's an excellent book of moral philosophy, madam, of Reynard the Fox and all the beasts, called *Doni's Philosophy.* 75

Centaure. There is indeed, Sir Amorous La Foole.

Morose. O misery!

La Foole. I have read it, my Lady Centaure, all over to my cousin here.

59–64 DISEASE . . . DELIRIUM *N.*

59 μανία *mania.*

62 LECTURE . . . ALIVE *become pedagogical subject matter, anatomized while still living.*

74–75 DONI'S PHILOSOPHY *N.*

80 *Mrs. Otter.* Ay, and 'tis a very good book as any is of the moderns.

  Daw. Tut, he must have Seneca read to him, and Plutarch and the ancients; the moderns are not for this disease.

  Clerimont. Why, you discommended them too today, Sir John.

  Daw. Ay, in some cases; but in these they are best, and Aristotle's
85 *Ethics.*

  Mavis. Say you so, Sir John? I think you are deceived; you took it upon trust.

  Haughty. Where's Trusty, my woman? I'll end this difference. I prithee, Otter, call her. Her father and mother were both mad,
90 when they put her to me. [*Exit Mrs. Otter.*]

  Morose. I think so. Nay, gentlemen, I am tame. This is but an exercise, I know, a marriage ceremony, which I must endure.

  Haughty. And one of 'em, I know not which, was cured with the *Sick Man's Salve*, and the other with Greene's *Groat's-worth of Wit.*
95 *Truewit.* A very cheap cure, madam.

      [*Enter Trusty and Mrs. Otter.*]

  Haughty. Ay, it's very feasible.

  Mrs. Otter. My lady called for you, Mistress Trusty; you must decide a controversy.

  Haughty. O, Trusty, which was it you said, your father or your
100 mother, that was cured with the *Sick Man's Salve?*

  Trusty. My mother, madam, with the *Salve.*

---

90 PUT . . . ME *placed her in my charge.*

92 EXERCISE *practice of a ceremony; training (of an animal: picking up implication of "tame," domesticated).*

93 ONE OF 'EM *i.e., of Trusty's parents.*

94 SICK MAN'S SALVE *a religious tract by the Calvinist Thomas Becon, first published in 1561 and frequently reprinted.*

 GREENE'S . . . WIT *a hortatory and confessional pamphlet (1592), the last of the cheap and immensely popular exposés of London low-life by the "University wit" and playwright, Robert Greene.*

Truewit. Then it was the *Sick Woman's Salve.*

Trusty. And my father with the *Groat's-worth of Wit.* But there was other means used: we had a preacher that would preach folk asleep still; and so they were prescribed to go to church, by an old woman that was their physician, thrice a week— 105

Epicoene. To sleep?

Trusty. Yes, forsooth; and every night they read themselves asleep on those books.

Epicoene. Good faith, it stands with great reason. I would I knew where to procure those books. 110

Morose. Oh!

La Foole. I can help you with one of 'em, Mistress Morose, the *Groat's-worth of Wit.*

Epicoene. But I shall disfurnish you, Sir Amorous. Can you spare it? 115

La Foole. O, yes, for a week or so; I'll read it myself to him.

Epicoene. No, I must do that, sir; that must be my office.

Morose. Oh, oh!

Epicoene. Sure, he would do well enough, if he could sleep. 120

Morose. No, I should do well enough if you could sleep. Have I no friend that will make her drunk, or give her a little laudanum, or opium?

Truewit. Why, sir, she talks ten times worse in her sleep.

Morose. How! 125

Clerimont. Do you not know that, sir? Never ceases all night.

Truewit. And snores like a porcpisce.

Morose. O, redeem me, fate, redeem me, fate! For how many causes may a man be divorced, nephew?

Dauphine. I know not truly, sir. 130

---

115 DISFURNISH *deprive you* (*of your Groat's-worth of Wit*).
127 PORCPISCE *porpoise* (*lit.*, "*pig-fish*").

Act IV Scene 4

Truewit. Some divine must resolve you in that, sir, or canon lawyer.

Morose. I will not rest, I will not think of any other hope or comfort till I know. [*Exit with Dauphine.*]

135 *Clerimont.* Alas, poor man!

Truewit. You'll make him mad indeed, ladies, if your pursue this.

Haughty. No, we'll let him breathe now, a quarter of an hour or so.

Clerimont. By my faith, a large truce.

140 *Haughty.* Is that his keeper that is gone with him?

Daw. It is his nephew, madam.

La Foole. Sir Dauphine Eugenie.

Centaure. He looks like a very pitiful knight—

Daw. As can be. This marriage has put him out of all.

145 *La Foole.* He has not a penny in his purse, madam—

Daw. He is ready to cry all this day.

La Foole. A very shark, he set me i' the nick t'other night at primero.

Truewit. [*Aside.*] How these swabbers talk!

150 *Clerimont.* [*Aside.*] Ay, Otter's wine has swelled their humours above a spring-tide.

Haughty. Good Morose, let's go in again. I like your couches exceeding well; we'll go lie and talk there.

Epicoene. I wait on you, madam.

[*Exeunt Haughty, Centaure, Mavis, Trusty, La Foole, and Daw.*]

131 RESOLVE . . . THAT *see IV.5.3–4 and fn.*

131–32 CANON LAWYER *one skilled in the rules (canons) of doctrine and discipline comprising the Corpus Juris Canonici (see II.3.73–74 and fn.), the body of law governing the Church and all matters subject to its jurisdiction.*

140 KEEPER *nurse.*

147 SHARK *crooked gambler.*

147–48 SET . . . PRIMERO *N.*

149 SWABBERS *term of contempt: "miserable louts."*

154 I . . . YOU *I (shall) attend you.*

Truewit. 'Slight, I will have 'em as silent as signs, and their posts 155
too, ere I ha' done. Do you hear, lady-bride? I pray thee now, as
thou art a noble wench, continue this discourse of Dauphine within;
but praise him exceedingly. Magnify him with all the height of
affection thou canst—I have some purpose in't—and but beat off
these two rooks, Jack Daw and his fellow, with any discontentment 160
hither, and I'll honor thee forever.

Epicoene. I was about it here. It angered me to the soul to hear 'em
begin to talk so malapert.

Truewit. Pray thee perform it, and thou winn'st me an idolater
to thee everlasting. 165

Epicoene. Will you go in and hear me do it?

Truewit. No, I'll stay here. Drive 'em out of your company, 'tis
all I ask, which cannot be any way better done than by extolling
Dauphine, whom they have so slighted.

Epicoene. I warrant you; you shall expect one of 'em presently. 170
[*Exit.*]

Clerimont. What a cast of kestrels are these, to hawk after ladies,
thus!

Truewit. Ay, and strike at such an eagle as Dauphine.

Clerimont. He will be mad when we tell him. Here he comes.

155 POSTS *i.e., poles for displaying signs.*
159 BEAT OFF *drive away.*
162 ABOUT IT *on the point of it.*
163 MALAPERT *(quasi-adverb) impudent. (OED.)*
171 CAST *in hawking, the number of hawks cast off at a time, usually two.*
KESTRELS *see I.4.69 and fn.*

Act IV Scene 5

[*Enter Dauphine.*]

Clerimont. O, sir, you are welcome.

Truewit. Where's thine uncle?

Dauphine. Run out o' doors in's nightcaps to talk with a casuist about his divorce. It works admirably.

5   *Truewit.* Thou wouldst ha' said so an' thou hadst been here! The ladies have laughed at thee most comically since thou went'st, Dauphine.

Clerimont. And asked if thou wert thine uncle's keeper?

Truewit. And the brace of baboons answered, "Yes," and said thou

10 wert a pitiful poor fellow and didst live upon posts, and hadst nothing but three suits of apparel, and some few benevolences that lords ga' thee to fool to 'em and swagger.

Dauphine. Let me not live, I'll beat 'em. I'll bind 'em both to grand madam's bed-posts, and have 'em baited with monkeys.

15   *Truewit.* Thou shalt not need, they shall be beaten to thy hand, Dauphine. I have an execution to serve upon 'em, I warrant thee, shall serve; trust my plot.

Dauphine. Ay, you have many plots! So you had one to make all the wenches in love with me.

3 CASUIST *one who resolves cases of conscience or doubtful questions concerning duty or conduct; often used with a suggestion of sophistry.*

10 UPON POSTS *by running errands.*

11 THREE SUITS *the usual number for servants.*
    BENEVOLENCES *gifts (for the support of the poor).*

12 TO FOOL TO *play the buffoon for.*

15 BEATEN . . . HAND *driven by blows into your power.*

16 EXECUTION *see II.5.93 and fn. Truewit, as sheriff, will enforce the judgment of the "court" by taking Daw and La Foole into custody.*

Truewit. Why, if I do not yet afore night, as near as 'tis, and that   20
they do not every one invite thee and be ready to scratch for thee,
take the mortgage of my wit.

Clerimont. 'Fore God, I'll be his witness; thou shalt have it,
Dauphine; thou shalt be his fool for ever if thou dost not.

Truewit. Agreed. Perhaps 'twill be the better estate. Do you   25
observe this gallery, or rather lobby, indeed? Here are a couple of
studies, at each end one; here will I act such a tragi-comedy between
the Guelphs and the Ghibellines, Daw and La Foole. Which of 'em
comes out first will I seize on. You two shall be the chorus behind
the arras, and whip out between the acts and speak. If I do not make   30
'em keep the peace for this remnant of the day, if not of the year, I
have failed once—I hear Daw coming. Hide, and do not laugh, for
God's sake.   *[Dauphine and
                                                              Clerimont hide.]*

[*Enter Daw.*]

Daw. Which is the way into the garden, trow?

Truewit. O, Jack Daw! I am glad I have met with you. In good   35
faith, I must have this matter go no further between you. I must
ha' it taken up.

---

21 scratch] search F₂, F₃.

---

21 SCRATCH "*struggle fiercely to obtain*" (OED).
24 THOU *that is, Truewit.*
   HIS FOOL *i.e., the butt of Dauphine's jokes.*
25 ESTATE *share, interest, as in property: Dauphine would profit more from a
   proprietary interest in Truewit as his "fool" than in the ladies as his lovers.*
26–27 A COUPLE OF STUDIES *on which the two side doors of the stage open. Daw is
   put up in one at l. 72; La Foole in the other at l. 193.*
28 GUELPHS . . . GHIBELLINES *factions contending for power in Italy during the late
   Middle Ages: the former, the papal party; the latter, the imperial.*
30 ARRAS *a decorative tapestry, often projecting from the wall far enough to allow
   space for eavesdropping.*
34 TROW *abb. "trow you": do you think?*
37 TAKEN UP *made up.*

Daw. What matter, sir? Between whom?

Truewit. Come, you disguise it—Sir Amorous and you. If you
40 love me, Jack, you shall make use of your philosophy now, for
this once, and deliver me your sword. This is not the wedding the
Centaurs were at, though there be a she-one here. The bride has
entreated me I will see no blood shed at her bridal; you saw her
whisper me erewhile. [*Takes his sword.*]

45 *Daw.* As I hope to finish Tacitus, I intend no murder.

Truewit. Do you not wait for Sir Amorous?

Daw. Not I, by my knighthood.

Truewit. And your scholarship too?

Daw. And my scholarship too.

50 *Truewit.* Go to, then I return you your sword, and ask you mercy;
but put it not up, for you will be assaulted. I understood that you
had apprehended it, and walked here to brave him, and that you had
held your life contemptible in regard of your honor.

Daw. No, no, no such thing, I assure you. He and I parted now as
55 good friends as could be.

Truewit. Trust not you to that visor. I saw him since dinner with
another face. I have known many men in my time vexed with losses,
with deaths, and with abuses, but so offended a wight as Sir Amorous
did I never see, or read of. For taking away his guests, sir, today,
60 that's the cause, and he declares it behind your back with such
threatenings and contempts. He said to Dauphine you were the
arrant'st ass—

Daw. Ay, he may say his pleasure.

Truewit. And swears you are so protested a coward that he knows

42 CENTAURS *N.*

44 EREWHILE *a while before.*

52 APPREHENDED IT *understood that you would be assaulted.*
    BRAVE *challenge, defy.*

56 VISOR *false "face" (but anticipating the armory in ll. 96 ff.?).*

58 WIGHT *person.*

64 PROTESTED *avowed, notorious.*

you will never do him any manly or single right, and therefore he   65
will take his course.

Daw. I'll give him any satisfaction, sir—but fighting.

Truewit. Ay, sir, but who knows what satisfaction he'll take?
Blood he thirsts for, and blood he will have; and whereabouts on
you he will have it, who knows but himself?   70

Daw. I pray you, Master Truewit, be you a mediator.

Truewit. Well, sir, conceal yourself then in this study *He puts him up.*
till I return. Nay, you must be content to be locked in; for, for
mine own reputation, I would not have you seen to receive a public disgrace, while I have the matter in managing. Gods so, here he   75
comes; keep your breath close that he do not hear you sigh. [*In a
loud voice.*] In good faith, Sir Amorous, he is not this way; I pray
you, be merciful, do not murder him; he is a Christian as good as
you; you are armed as if you sought a revenge on all his race. Good
Dauphine, get him away from this place. I never knew a man's   80
choler so high, but he would speak to his friends, he would hear
reason. Jack Daw. Jack Daw! Asleep?

Daw. [*Within.*] Is he gone, Master Truewit?

Truewit. Ay, did you hear him?

Daw. O God, yes.   85

Truewit. [*Aside.*] What a quick ear fear has!

Daw. [*Comes out of the study.*] And is he so armed as you say?

Truewit. Armed? Did you ever see a fellow set out to take
possession?

Daw. Ay, sir.   90

Truewit. That may give you some light to conceive of him; but
'tis nothing to the principal. Some false brother i' the house has

---

65 DO . . . RIGHT *treat him justly, offer him satisfaction in honorable combat.*

SINGLE *man-to-man, as in a duel; also sincere, without duplicity.*

88–89 SET . . . POSSESSION *N.*

91 SOME . . . HIM *some idea of how to picture him.*

92 PRINCIPAL *original: i.e., what the heavily armed La Foole really looks like.*

furnished him strangely. Or, if it were out o' the house, it was Tom Otter.

95   *Daw*. Indeed, he's a Captain, and his wife is his kinswoman.

    Truewit. He has got somebody's old two-hand sword, to mow you off at the knees. And that sword hath spawned such a dagger!— but then he is so hung with pikes, halberds, petronels, calivers, and muskets, that he looks like a Justice of Peace's hall; a man of two 100 thousand a year is not sessed at so many weapons as he has on. There was never fencer challenged at so many several foils. You would think he meant to murder all Saint Pulchre's parish. If he could but victual himself for half a year in his breeches, he is sufficiently armed to overrun a country.

105   *Daw*. Good lord, what means he, sir? I pray you Master Truewit, be you a mediator.

    Truewit. Well, I'll try if he will be appeased with a leg or an arm; if not, you must die once.

    Daw. I would be loth to lose my right arm, for writing 110 madrigals.

93 STRANGELY *extraordinarily—i.e., with many kinds of weapons.*

95 HIS . . . KINSWOMAN *i.e., Otter's wife is La Foole's kinswoman.*

96 TWO-HAND SWORD *the old-fashioned broadsword, used rather like an axe.*

98 PIKES, HALBERDS *basic arms of the infantry, not dueling weapons; the pike was a shaft often sixteen feet long with a point for thrusting; the halberd, somewhat shorter, had a point, axe-head, and hook (for pulling down horsemen).*
    PETRONELS *heavy pistols or carbines.*
    CALIVERS *light muskets.*

99 JUSTICE . . . HALL *conventionally used as a weapons museum and an armory.*

99–100 MAN . . . YEAR *N.*

100 SESSED *aphetic for "assessed".*

101 AT . . . FOILS *to defend himself (fence) against so wide a choice of weapons.*

102 SAINT PULCHRE'S PARISH *St. Sepulchre's, a crowded and noisome part of the city near Newgate.*

103 VICTUAL . . . BREECHES *fashionable Jacobean breeches were so fully pleated and stuffed that Truewit pictures La Foole using his as a commissary.*

108 ONCE *at once? in any case?*

Truewit. Why, if he will be satisfied with a thumb or a little finger, all's one to me. You must think I'll do my best.

Daw. Good sir, do.

[*Truewit*] *puts him up again, and then* [*Clerimont and Dauphine come forth.*]

Clerimont. What hast thou done?

Truewit. He will let me do nothing, man, he does all afore me; he   115
offers his left arm.

Clerimont. His left wing, for a Jack Daw.

Dauphine. Take it, by all means.

Truewit. How! Maim a man forever for a jest? What a conscience hast thou!   120

Dauphine. 'Tis no loss to him; he has no employment for his arms
but to eat spoon-meat. Besides, as good maim his body as his
reputation.

Truewit. He is a scholar and a wit, and yet he does not think so.
But he loses no reputation with us, for we all resolved him an ass   125
before. To your places again.

Clerimont. I pray thee, let me be in at the other a little.

Truewit. Look, you'll spoil all; these be ever your tricks.

Clerimont. No, but I could hit of some things that thou wilt miss,
and thou wilt say are good ones.   130

Truewit. I warrant you. I pray, forbear, I'll leave it off else.

Dauphine. Come away, Clerimont. [*They withdraw again.*]
[*Enter La Foole.*]

Truewit. Sir Amorous!

La Foole. Master Truewit.

Truewit. Whither were you going?   135

122 SPOON-MEAT *soft or liquid food eaten with a spoon, especially by infants and invalids.*

125 RESOLVED HIM *decided he was.*

127 BE . . . OTHER *i.e., take part in fooling La Foole.*

129 HIT OF *light on.*

Act IV Scene 5

La Foole. Down into the court to make water.

Truewit. By no means, sir; you shall rather tempt your breeches.

La Foole. Why, sir?

Truewit. Enter here if you love your life. [*Opening the door to the*
140 *other study.*]

La Foole. Why? Why?

Truewit. Question till your throat be cut, do; dally till the
enraged soul find you.

La Foole. Who's that?

145 *Truewit.* Daw it is. Will you in?

La Foole. Ay, ay, I'll in. What's the matter?

Truewit. Nay, if he had been cool enough to tell us that, there had
been some hope to atone you, but he seems so implacably enraged!

La Foole. 'Slight, let him rage. I'll hide myself.

150 *Truewit.* Do, good sir. But what have you done to him within
that should provoke him thus? You have broke some jest upon him
afore the ladies—

La Foole. Not I, [I] never in my life broke jest upon any man. The
bride was praising Sir Dauphine, and he went away in snuff, and I
155 followed him, unless he took offence at me in his drink erewhile,
that I would not pledge all the horse full.

Truewit. By my faith, and that may be, you remember well; but
he walks the round up and down, through every room o' the house,
with a towel in his hand, crying, "Where's La Foole? Who saw La
160 Foole?" And when Dauphine and I demanded the cause, we can
force no answer from him but "O revenge, how sweet art thou!

137 TEMPT YOUR BREECHES *put your breeches to the test.*

148 ATONE *reconcile (to set "at one").*

151 BROKE SOME JEST *cracked a joke.*

154 IN SNUFF *offended: in a huff.*

156 PLEDGE . . . FULL *In IV.2.14–38 La Foole, who was drinking from the "horse,"*
at first refused to empty his cup.

158 WALKS THE ROUND *as of a sentry post.*

I will strangle him in this towel"—which leads us to conjecture that the main cause of his fury is for bringing your meat today, with a towel about you, to his discredit.

La Foole. Like enough. Why, an' he be angry for that, I'll stay 165 here till his anger be blown over.

Truewit. A good becoming resolution, sir. If you can put it on o' the sudden.

La Foole. Yes, I can put it on. Or I'll away into the country presently. 170

Truewit. How will you get out o' the house, sir? He knows you are i' the house, and he'll watch you this se'n-night but he'll have you. He'll outwait a sergeant for you.

La Foole. Why, then I'll stay here.

Truewit. You must think how to victual yourself in time then. 175

La Foole. Why, sweet Master Truewit, will you entreat my cousin Otter to send me a cold venison pasty, a bottle or two of wine, and a chamber pot?

Truewit. A stool were better, sir, of Sir Ajax his invention.

La Foole. Ay, that will be better indeed, and a pallet to lie on. 180

Truewit. O, I would not advise you to sleep by any means.

La Foole. Would you not, sir? Why, then I will not.

Truewit. Yet there's another fear—

La Foole. Is there, sir? What is't?

Truewit. No, he cannot break open this door with his foot, sure. 185

179 Ajax] A-jax F.

---

169 PUT IT ON *adopt or assume a character. La Foole apparently misses the ironic criticism implied by* "resolution".

172 SE'N-NIGHT *a week.*

173 SERGEANT *officer who could serve summonses and subpoenas, and was empowered to make arrests.*

179 AJAX . . . INVENTION *a pun on* "*a jakes*" (*a privy*), *made popular by* The Metamorphosis of Ajax (1596), *Sir John Harington's tract on a toilet that flushed, the* "*invention*" *recommended to La Foole for a long stay.*

La Foole. I'll set my back against it, sir. I have a good back.

Truewit. But then if he should batter.

La Foole. Batter! If he dare, I'll have an action of batt'ry against him.

190   *Truewit.* Cast you the worst. He has sent for powder already, and what he will do with it, no man knows; perhaps blow up the corner o' the house where he suspects you are. Here he comes; in quickly. [*Raising his voice.*] I protest, Sir John Daw, he is not this way; what will you do? Before God you shall hang no *He feigns, as if*
195 petard here. I'll die rather. Will you not take my *one were present,*
word? I never knew one but would be satisfied. Sir *to fright the*
Amorous, there's no standing out. He has made a *other, who is run*
in to hide himself.
petard of an old brass pot, to force your door. Think upon some satisfaction or terms to offer him.

200   *La Foole.* [*Within.*] Sir, I'll give him any satisfaction. I dare give any terms.

Truewit. You'll leave it to me then?

La Foole. Ay, sir. I'll stand to any conditions.

           [*Truewit*] *calls forth Clerimont and Dauphine.*

Truewit. How now, what think you, sirs? Were't not a difficult
205 thing to determine which of these two feared most?

Clerimont. Yes, but this fears the bravest: the other a whiniling dastard, Jack Daw. But La Foole, a brave heroic coward! And is afraid in a great look and a stout accent. I like him rarely.

187 BATTER *as with a battering-ram.*

190 CAST *anticipate (forecast).*

195 PETARD *bomb or mine.*

197 STANDING OUT *resisting.*

203 STAND TO *he means "submit" but hopes it will sound like resolution: e.g.,*
    face fearlessly (stand up to), or maintain with integrity (stand by).

206 THIS *La Foole.*

    BRAVEST *i.e., with the most bravado.*

    WHINILING *whimpering.*

Truewit. Had it not been pity these two should ha' been concealed? 210

Clerimont. Shall I make a motion?

Truewit. Briefly. For I must strike while 'tis hot.

Clerimont. Shall I go fetch the ladies to the catastrophe?

Truewit. Umh? Ay, by my troth.

Dauphine. By no mortal means. Let them continue in the state of 215 ignorance, and err still; think 'em wits and fine fellows as they have done. 'Twere sin to reform them.

Truewit. Well, I will have 'em fetched, now I think on't, for a private purpose of mine; do, Clerimont, fetch 'em, and discourse to 'em all that's passed, and bring 'em into the gallery here. 220

Dauphine. This is thy extreme vanity now; thou think'st thou wert undone if every jest thou mak'st were not published.

Truewit. Thou shalt see how unjust thou art presently. Clerimont, say it was Dauphine's plot. [*Exit Clerimont.*] Trust me not if the whole drift be not for thy good. There's a carpet i' the next room, 225 put it on, with this scarf over thy face, and a cushion o' thy head, and be ready when I call Amorous. Away! [*Exit Dauphine.*] John Daw!

[*Daw peeps out of his study.*]

Daw. What good news, sir?

Truewit. [*Bringing Daw out.*] Faith, I have followed and argued 230 with him hard for you. I told him you were a knight and a scholar, and that you knew fortitude did consist *magis patiendo quam faciendo, magis ferendo quam feriendo.*

Daw. It doth so indeed, sir.

---

211 MOTION *suggestion.*
213 CATASTROPHE *denouement.*
225 CARPET *tablecloth.*
232–33 MAGIS . . . FERIENDO *more in suffering than in doing, more in enduring than in striking a blow. N.*

235 *Truewit.* And that you would suffer, I told him: so at first he demanded, by my troth, in my conceit, too much.

Daw. What was it, sir?

Truewit. Your upper lip, and six o' your fore-teeth.

Daw. 'Twas unreasonable.

240 *Truewit.* Nay, I told him plainly, you could not spare 'em all. So after long argument—pro and con, as you know—I brought him down to your two butter-teeth, and them he would have.

Daw. O, did you so? Why, he shall have 'em.

[*Enter, above, Haughty, Centaure, Mavis, Mistress Otter, Epicoene, Clerimont and Trusty.*]

Truewit. But he shall not, sir, by your leave. The conclusion is

245 this, sir, because you shall be very good friends hereafter, and this never to be remembered or upbraided, besides that he may not boast he has done any such thing to you in his own person: he is to come here in disguise, give you five kicks in private, sir, take your sword from you, and lock you up in that study during pleasure. Which

250 will be but a little while, we'll get it released presently.

Daw. Five kicks? He shall have six, sir, to be friends.

Truewit. Believe me, you shall not overshoot yourself to send him that word by me.

Daw. Deliver it, sir. He shall have it with all my heart, to be

255 friends.

Truewit. Friends? Nay, an' he should not be so, and heartily too, upon these terms, he shall have me to enemy while I live. Come, sir, bear it bravely.

Daw. O God, sir, 'tis nothing.

236 CONCEIT *opinion, judgment.*

242 BUTTER-TEETH *front teeth (H & S).*

245 BECAUSE *in order that.*

249 DURING PLEASURE *so long as he pleases.*

252 OVERSHOOT *make any mistake.*

Truewit. True. What's six kicks to a man that reads Seneca?   260

Daw. I have had a hundred, sir.

Truewit. [*To Dauphine.*] Sir Amorous. No speaking one to another, or rehearsing old matters.

                    Dauphine comes forth and kicks him.

Daw. One, two, three, four, five. I protest, Sir Amorous, you shall have six.   265

Truewit. Nay, I told you, you should not talk. Come, give him six, an' he will needs. [*Dauphine kicks him again.*] Your sword. [*Takes his sword.*] Now return to your safe custody: you shall presently meet afore the ladies, and be the dearest friends one to another. [*Daw returns to the study. To Dauphine.*] Give me the scarf; now thou   270 shalt beat the other barefaced. Stand by—[*Dauphine withdraws; Truewit calls to La Foole.*] Sir Amorous.

La Foole. [*Entering.*] What's here? A sword!

Truewit. I cannot help it, without I should take the quarrel upon myself. Here he has sent you his sword—   275

La Foole. I'll receive none on't.

Truewit. And he wills you to fasten it against a wall, and break your head in some few several places against the hilts.

La Foole. I will not: tell him roundly. I cannot endure to shed my own blood.   280

Truewit. Will you not?

La Foole. No. I'll beat it against a fair flat wall, if that will satisfy him. If not, he shall beat it himself, for Amorous.

Truewit. Why, this is strange starting off when a man undertakes for you! I offered him another condition. Will you stand to that?   285

La Foole. Ay, what is't?

260 SENECA *here as a Stoic philosopher. See II.3.40–42. N.*

274 WITHOUT *unless.*

278 HILTS *the transverse projections where the handle joins the blade.*

283 FOR AMOROUS *for all Amorous cares.*

284 UNDERTAKES *takes up a matter.*

Truewit. That you will be beaten in private.

La Foole. Yes. I am content, at the blunt.

Truewit. Then you must submit yourself to be hood-winked in
290 this scarf, and be led to him, where he will take your sword from
you, and make you bear a blow over the mouth *gules*, and tweaks
by the nose *sans nombre*.

La Foole. I am content. But why must I be blinded?

Truewit. That's for your good, sir: because if he should grow
295 insolent upon this and publish it hereafter to your disgrace—which
I hope he will not do—you might swear safely and protest he
never beat you, to your knowledge.

La Foole. O, I conceive.

Truewit. I do not doubt but you'll be perfect good friends
300 upon't, and not dare to utter an ill thought one of another in future.

La Foole. Not I, as God help me, of him.

Truewit. Nor he of you, sir. If he should—[*Covers his eyes.*] Come,
sir. [*Calling to Dauphine.*] All hid, Sir John.

> *Dauphine enters to tweak him.*

La Foole. Oh, Sir John, Sir John. Oh, o-o-o-o-o-Oh—

305 *Truewit.* Good Sir John, leave tweaking, you'll blow his nose off.
[*To La Foole.*] 'Tis Sir John's pleasure you should retire into the
study. Why, now you are friends. All bitterness between you, I
hope, is buried; you shall come forth by and by, Damon and
Pythias upon't, and embrace with all the rankness of friendship that

288 AT THE BLUNT *with the sword-point covered by a button, thus harmless; or*
possibly, with the flat of the sword.

289 HOOD-WINKED *blindfolded (and deceived?)*

291 MAKE . . . GULES *i.e., "give you a bloody mouth", with a quibble on gullet (Latin*
gula) *and the heraldic color, red.*

295 PUBLISH IT *tell it around. See ll. 221–22.*

298 CONCEIVE *understand.*

308–09 DAMON AND PYTHIAS *N.*

309 UPON'T *concerning the quarrel.*
RANKNESS *exuberance; but an ironic play on "foulness".*

can be. [*Puts La Foole into the study.*] I trust we shall have 'em tamer   310
i' their language hereafter. Dauphine, I worship thee. God's will, the
ladies have surprised us!

Act IV Scene 6

*Haughty, Centaure, Mavis, Mrs. Otter, Epicoene, Trusty, [and Clerimont
enter] having discovered part of the past scene, above.*

Haughty. Centaure, how our judgments were imposed on by these
adulterate knights!

Centaure. Nay, madam, Mavis was more deceived than we; 'twas
her commendation utter'd 'em in the college.

Mavis. I commended but their wits, madam, and their braveries.   5
I never looked toward their valors.

Haughty. Sir Dauphine is valiant and a Wit too, it seems.

Mavis. And a Bravery too.

Haughty. Was this his project?

Mrs. Otter. So Master Clerimont intimates, madam.   10

Haughty. Good Morose, when you come to the college, will
you bring him with you? He seems a very perfect gentleman.

Epicoene. He is so, madam, believe it.

Centaure. But when will you come, Morose?

Epicoene. Three or four days hence, madam, when I have got me   15
a coach and horses.

Haughty. No, tomorrow, good Morose; Centaure shall send you
her coach.

1 SD HAVING DISCOVERED *N.*

2 ADULTERATE *counterfeit.*

4 UTTER'D 'EM *put Daw and La Foole into circulation.*

5 BRAVERIES *fine attire; see I.1.71 fn.*

Act IV Scene 6

Mavis. Yes, faith, do, and bring Sir Dauphine with you.

20 *Haughty.* She has promised that, Mavis.

Mavis. He is a very worthy gentleman in his exteriors, madam.

Haughty. Ay, he shows he is judicial in his clothes.

Centaure. And yet not so superlatively neat as some, madam, that have their faces set in a brake!

25 *Haughty.* Ay, and have every hair in form!

Mavis. That wear purer linen than ourselves, and profess more neatness than the French hermaphrodite!

Epicoene. Ay, ladies, they, what they tell one of us, have told a thousand, and are the only thieves of our fame, that think to take

30 us with that perfume or with that lace, and laugh at us unconscionably when they have done.

Haughty. But Sir Dauphine's carelessness becomes him.

Centaure. I could love a man for such a nose!

Mavis. Or such a leg!

35 *Centaure.* He has an exceeding good eye, madam!

Mavis. And a very good lock!

Centaure. Good Morose, bring him to my chamber first.

Mrs. Otter. Please your honors to meet at my house, madam?

Truewit. [*Aside to Dauphine.*] See how they eye thee, man! They

40 are taken, I warrant thee.

Haughty. [*Comes forward.*] You have unbraced our brace of knights here, Master Truewit.

24 FACES . . . BRAKE *a brake was a framework designed to hold anything steady, such as a horse's hoof when being shod; hence, faces which have assumed a stylized or frozen look.*

27 FRENCH HERMAPHRODITE *1. a double figure of "neatness"—that is, elegant dress— because he is French (see II.5.63 and fn.) and effeminate (see I.1.73). 2. "a sideshow" (Six Elizabethan Plays, ed. R. C. Bald [Boston, 1963]). 3. "King Henry III of France, a notorious transvestite, subject of Thomas Arthus' Isle des Hermaphrodites (1605)" (Beaurline).*

36 LOCK *a love-lock. See III.5.61 and fn.*

41 UNBRACED *exposed, disarmed, made feeble.*

140

Truewit. Not I, madam; it was Sir Dauphine's engine: who, if he have disfurnished your ladyship of any guard or service by it, is able to make the place good again in himself.　　　　　　　　45

Haughty. [*Approaching Dauphine.*] There's no suspicion of that, sir.

Centaure. God so, Mavis, Haughty is kissing.

Mavis. Let us go too and take part. [*They come forward.*]

Haughty. But I am glad of the fortune—beside the discovery of two such empty caskets—to gain the knowledge of so rich a mine　　50 of virtue as Sir Dauphine.

Centaure. We would be all glad to style him of our friendship, and see him at the college.

Mavis. He cannot mix with a sweeter society, I'll prophesy, and I hope he himself will think so.　　　　　　　　55

Dauphine. I should be rude to imagine otherwise, lady.

Truewit. [*Aside to Dauphine.*] Did not I tell thee, Dauphine? Why, all their actions are governed by crude opinion, without reason or cause; they know not why they do anything; but as they are informed, believe, judge, praise, condemn, love, hate, and in　　60 emulation one of another, do all these things alike. Only, they have a natural inclination sways 'em generally to the worst, when they are left to themselves. But pursue it, now thou hast 'em.

Haughty. Shall we go in again, Morose?

Epicoene. Yes, madam.　　　　　　　　65

Centaure. We'll entreat Sir Dauphine's company.

Truewit. Stay, good madam, the interview of the two friends, Pylades and Orestes: I'll fetch 'em out to you straight.

Haughty. Will you, Master Truewit?

43　ENGINE *plot.*

44　DISFURNISHED *see IV.4.115 and fn.*

46　SUSPICION *expectation* (*that Dauphine would not be able to take the place of Daw and La Foole*).

67　STAY *stay for; remain and witness.*

68　PYLADES AND ORESTES *N.*

70   *Dauphine.* Ay, but, noble ladies, do not confess in your countenance or outward bearing to 'em any discovery of their follies, that we may see how they will bear up again, with what assurance and erection.

    Haughty. We will not, Sir Dauphine.

75   *Centaure. Mavis.* Upon our honors, Sir Dauphine.

    Truewit. [*Goes to the study.*] Sir Amorous, Sir Amorous. The ladies are here.

    La Foole. [*Within.*] Are they?

    Truewit. Yes, but slip out by and by as their backs are turned and
80 meet Sir John here, as by chance, when I call you. [*Goes to the other.*] Jack Daw.

    Daw. What say you, sir?

    Truewit. Whip out behind me suddenly, and no anger i' your looks to your adversary. Now, now!

        [*La Foole and Daw enter and greet each other.*]

85   *La Foole.* Noble Sir John Daw! Where ha' you been?

    Daw. To seek you, Sir Amorous.

    La Foole. Me! I honor you.

    Daw. I prevent you, sir.

    Clerimont. They have forgot their rapiers!

90   *Truewit.* O, they meet in peace, man.

    Dauphine. Where's your sword, Sir John?

    Clerimont. And yours, Sir Amorous?

    Daw. Mine? My boy had it forth to mend the handle, e'en now.

    La Foole. And my gold handle was broke too, and my boy had it
95 forth.

    Dauphine. Indeed, sir? How their excuses meet!

    Clerimont. What a consent there is i' the handles!

---

73 ERECTION *exaltation of spirit; "high spirits"; possibly, for the Collegiates, an erotic allusion too.*

88 PREVENT *anticipate.*

97 CONSENT *agreement, unity of opinion.*

Truewit. Nay, there is so i' the points too, I warrant you.

Mrs. Otter. O me! Madam, he comes again, the madman! Away!

[*They all run off, except Truewit, Clerimont, and Dauphine.*]

99 Mrs. Otter] Mrs. Ot. F₁; Mrs. T. H & S.

Act IV Scene 7

[*Enter Morose, with the two swords.*]   *He had found*
the two swords
Morose. What make these naked weapons here,   *drawn within.*
gentlemen?

Truewit. O, sir! Here hath like to been murder since you went! A
couple of knights fallen out about the bride's favors. We were fain
to take away their weapons, your house had been begged by this   5
time else—

Morose. For what?

Clerimont. For manslaughter, sir, as being accessory.

Morose. And for her favors?

Truewit. Ay, sir, heretofore, not present. Clerimont, carry 'em   10
their swords now. They have done all the hurt they will do. [*Exit
Clerimont with the swords.*]

Dauphine. Ha' you spoke with a lawyer, sir?

Morose. O, no! There is such a noise i' the court that they have
frighted me home with more violence than I went! Such speaking   15

4 FAIN *obliged.*

5 BEGGED *N.*

10 HERETOFORE, NOT PRESENT *i.e., Daw and La Foole were quarreling about the
favors Epicoene granted before her marriage, not since.*

and counter-speaking, with their several voices of citations, appella-
tions, allegations, certificates, attachments, intergatories, references,
convictions, and afflictions indeed among the doctors and proctors,
that the noise here is silence to't! A kind of calm midnight!

20   *Truewit.* Why, sir, if you would be resolved indeed, I can bring
you hither a very sufficient lawyer and a learned divine, that shall
inquire into every least scruple for you.

  Morose. Can you, Master Truewit?

  Truewit. Yes, and are very sober grave persons, that will dispatch
25 it in a chamber, with a whisper or two.

  Morose. Good sir, shall I hope this benefit from you, and trust
myself into your hands?

  Truewit. Alas, sir! Your nephew and I have been ashamed, and
oft-times mad, since you went, to think how you are abused. Go in,
30 good sir, and lock yourself up till we call you; we'll tell you
more anon, sir.

  Morose. Do your pleasure with me, gentlemen; I believe in you,
and that deserves no delusion—[*Exit.*]

  Truewit. You shall find none, sir: but heaped, heaped plenty of
35 vexation.

  Dauphine. What wilt thou do now, Wit?

  Truewit. Recover me hither Otter and the barber if you can, by
any means, presently.

  Dauphine. Why? To what purpose?

40   *Truewit.* O, I'll make the deepest divine and gravest lawyer out o'
them two, for him—

  Dauphine. Thou canst not, man; these are waking dreams.

---

17 ATTACHMENTS *writs ordering the apprehension and legal confinement of a person.*
    INTERGATORIES *interrogatories.*
    REFERENCES *submitting disputes for settlement, especially in the Court of Chancery.*
18 DOCTORS *scholars proficient in the knowledge of the law.*
    PROCTORS *attorneys, strictly in the admiralty and ecclesiastical courts.*
22 SCRUPLE *fine distinction.*

Truewit. Do not fear me. Clap but a civil gown with a welt o' the one, and a canonical cloak with sleeves o' the other, and give 'em a few terms i' their mouths, if there come not forth as able a doc- 45 tor and complete a parson, for this turn, as may be wished, trust not my election. And, I hope, without wronging the dignity of either profession, since they are but persons put on, and for mirth's sake, to torment him. The barber smatters Latin, I remember.

Dauphine. Yes, and Otter too. 50

Truewit. Well, then, if I make 'em not wrangle out this case to his no comfort, let me be thought a Jack Daw, or La Foole, or anything worse. Go you to your ladies, but first send for them.

Dauphine. I will. [*Exeunt.*]

43 FEAR *doubt.*

43–44 CIVIL GOWN . . . CANONICAL CLOAK *Truewit is distinguishing the gown of the civil lawyer with its bordering ("welt") of fur or velvet from the sleeved cloak of the canon lawyer.*

46 TURN *occasion, purpose.*

47 ELECTION *discrimination.*

48 PUT ON *assumed or "acted." See* Another (Prologue), *ll. 11–14.*

53 THEM *i.e., Cutbeard and Otter.*

Act V Scene 1

[*Morose's house.*]

[*Enter La Foole, Daw, and Clerimont, with their swords.*]

La Foole. Where had you our swords, Master Clerimont?

Clerimont. Why, Dauphine took 'em from the madman.

La Foole. And he took 'em from our boys, I warrant you.

Clerimont. Very like, sir.

5   *La Foole.* Thank you, good Master Clerimont. Sir John Daw and I are both beholden to you.

Clerimont. Would I knew how to make you so, gentlemen.

Daw. Sir Amorous and I are your servants, sir.

[*Enter Mavis.*]

Mavis. Gentlemen, have any of you a pen and ink? I would
10   fain write out a riddle in Italian, for Sir Dauphine to translate.

Clerimont. Not I, in troth, lady, I am so scrivener.

Daw. I can furnish you, I think, lady.

Clerimont. He has it in the haft of a knife, I believe!

[*Exit Daw and Mavis.*]

La Foole. No, he has his box of instruments.

15   *Clerimont.* Like a surgeon!

---

11 SCRIVENER *professional scribe; the modern equivalent would be a stenographer or perhaps a law clerk. N.*

La Foole. For the mathematics: his squire, his compasses, his brass pens, and black lead, to draw maps of every place and person, where he comes.

Clerimont. How, maps of persons!

La Foole. Yes, sir, of Nomentack, when he was here, and of the Prince of Moldavia, and of his mistress, Mistress Epicoene. 20

Clerimont. Away! He has not found out her latitude, I hope.

La Foole. You are a pleasant gentleman, sir. [*Re-enter Daw.*]

Clerimont. Faith, now we are in private, let's wanton it a little, and talk waggishly. Sir John, I am telling Sir Amorous here that you two govern the ladies where'er you come; you carry the feminine 25 gender afore you.

Daw. They shall rather carry us afore them, if they will, sir.

Clerimont. Nay, I believe that they do, withal—but that you are the prime men in their affections, and direct all their actions— 30

Daw. Not I; Sir Amorous is.

La Foole. I protest, Sir John is.

Daw. As I hope to rise i' the state, Sir Amorous, you ha' the person.

La Foole. Sir John, you ha' the person, and the discourse too. 35

Daw. Not I, sir. I have no discourse—and then you have activity beside.

16 SQUIRE *square.*

20 NOMENTACK *an Indian chief of Virginia who was brought to England as a hostage in 1605; on his return trip he was murdered in Bermuda, apparently by another Indian.*

21 PRINCE OF MOLDAVIA *see Dedication N. and Appendix.* HIS *i.e., Daw's.*

22 LATITUDE *a quibble on geographical (l. 19) and moral meanings; latitude: freedom from narrow restrictions and even laxity of conduct. See "height" and "line" IV.1.85 and fn.*

23 PLEASANT *facetious.*

34 PERSON *role or function; perhaps physical attractiveness.*

36 ACTIVITY *see IV.1.90 and fn.*

147

Act V Scene 1

La Foole. I protest, Sir John, you come as high from Tripoli as I do every whit, and lift as many joined stools and leap over 'em, if
40 you would use it—

Clerimont. Well, agree on't together, knights, for between you, you divide the kingdom, or commonwealth, of ladies' affections. I see it and can perceive a little how they observe you and fear you, indeed. You could tell strange stories, my masters, if you would, I
45 know.

Daw. Faith, we have seen somewhat, sir.

La Foole. That we have—velvet petticoats and wrought smocks or so.

Daw. Ay, and—
50 *Clerimont.* Nay, out with it, Sir John; do not envy your friend the pleasure of hearing, when you have had the delight of tasting.

Daw. Why—a—do you speak, Sir Amorous.

La Foole. No, do you, Sir John Daw.

Daw. I' faith, you shall.
55 *La Foole.* I' faith, you shall.

Daw. Why, we have been—

La Foole. In the Great Bed at Ware together in our time. On, Sir John.

Daw. Nay, do you, Sir Amorous.
60 *Clerimont.* And these ladies with you, knights?

La Foole. No, excuse us, sir.

Daw. We must not wound reputation.

47 velvet] F₂; vellet F₁.

---

38 COME ... TRIPOLI *vault as energetically? Gifford thinks Tripoli is used simply because of the play on its first syllable. The phrase sounds like an allusion to a gymnastic exercise or a trick or even a game.*

40 USE *practice.*

47 VELVET ... SMOCKS *customarily worn by expensive prostitutes.*

57 GREAT BED AT WARE *a mammoth bed, nearly 11 feet square, built about 1580, already famous in 1609, and now in the Victoria and Albert Museum (London).*

La Foole. No matter—they were these, or others. Our bath cost us fifteen pound, when we came home.

Clerimont. Do you hear, Sir John, you shall tell me but one 65 thing truly, as you love me.

Daw. If I can, I will, sir.

Clerimont. You lay in the same house with the bride here?

Daw. Yes, and conversed with her hourly, sir.

Clerimont. And what humour is she of? Is she coming and open, 70 free?

Daw. O, exceeding open, sir. I was her servant, and Sir Amorous was to be.

Clerimont. Come, you have both had favors from her? I know and have heard so much. 75

Daw. O, no, sir.

La Foole. You shall excuse us, sir; we must not wound reputation.

Clerimont. Tut, she is married, now, and you cannot hurt her with any report, and therefore speak plainly: how many times, i'faith? Which of you led first? Ha? 80

La Foole. Sir John had her maidenhead, indeed.

Daw. O, it pleases him to say so, sir, but Sir Amorous knows what's what as well.

Clerimont. Dost thou i'faith, Amorous?

La Foole. In a manner, sir. 85

Clerimont. Why, I commend you, lads. Little knows Don Bridegroom of this. Nor shall he, for me.

Daw. Hang him, mad ox.

63 BATH *hot and medicinal, presumably to prevent venereal disease.*

68 LAY *lived; and a quibble on "had intercourse with."*

70 COMING *inclined to make or meet advances.*

72 SERVANT *lover.*

86 DON *the Spanish title for "Master" was often used contemptuously or jocularly, somewhat the way we now use "Comrade."*

88 MAD OX *i.e., the horned cuckold, enraged at his humiliating status.*

149

Clerimont. Speak softly; here comes his nephew, with the Lady
90 Haughty. He'll get the ladies from you, sirs, if you look not to him
in time.

La Foole. Why, if he do, we'll fetch 'em home again, I warrant
you. [*Exeunt.*]

90 LOOK NOT TO *do not keep watch on.*

Act V Scene 2

[*Enter Haughty and Dauphine.*]

Haughty. I assure you, Sir Dauphine, it is the price and estimation
of your virtue only that hath embarked me to this adventure, and I
could not but make out to tell you so; nor can I repent me of the
act, since it is always an argument of some virtue in ourselves that
5 we love and affect it so in others.

Dauphine. Your ladyship sets too high a price on my weakness.

Haughty. Sir, I can distinguish gems from pebbles—

Dauphine. [*Aside.*] Are you so skillful in stones?

Haughty. And howsoever I may suffer in such a judgment as yours,
10 by admitting equality of rank or society with Centaure or Mavis—

Dauphine. You do not, madam; I perceive they are your mere
foils.

1 PRICE . . . ESTIMATION *value and excellence.* N.

3 MAKE OUT *make a point of.*

5 AFFECT *desire, seek.*

8 SKILLFUL *knowledgeable, practiced.* STONES "*gems*"; *testicles.*

10 SOCIETY *association, familiarity.*

12 FOILS *setting for a jewel; something that enhances, sets off to advantage.*

Haughty. Then you are a friend to truth, sir. It makes me love you the more. It is not the outward but the inward man that I affect. They are not apprehensive of an eminent perfection, but love flat and 15
dully.

Centaure. [*Within.*] Where are you, my Lady Haughty?

Haughty. I come presently, Centaure. My chamber, sir, my page shall show you; and Trusty, my woman, shall be ever awake for you; you need not fear to communicate anything with her, for she 20
is a Fidelia. I pray you wear this jewel for my sake, Sir Dauphine. [*Enter Centaure.*] Where's Mavis, Centaure?

Centaure. Within, madam, a-writing. I'll follow you presently. I'll but speak a word with Sir Dauphine. [*Exit Haughty.*]

Dauphine. With me, madam? 25

Centaure. Good Sir Dauphine, do not trust Haughty, nor make any credit to her, whatever you do besides. Sir Dauphine, I give you this caution, she is a perfect courtier and loves nobody but for her uses, and for her uses, she loves all. Besides, her physicians give her out to be none o' the clearest—whether she pay 'em or no, 30
heaven knows; and she's above fifty too, and pargets! See her in a forenoon. Here comes Mavis, a worse face than she! You would not like this by candle-light. If you'll come to my chamber one o' these mornings early, or late in an evening, I'll tell you more. [*Enter Mavis.*] Where's Haughty, Mavis? 35

Mavis. Within, Centaure.

Centaure. What ha' you there?

Mavis. An Italian riddle for Sir Dauphine—you shall not see it

15–16 FLAT . . . DULLY *stupidly, as lacking sensitivity, spirit, or both.*
21 A FIDELIA *i.e., as faithful as the heroines of that name in popular romances; also a Latinizing of "Trusty."*
26–27 MAKE . . . HER *put any faith in her.*
30 CLEAREST *"purest" morally as well as medically.*
31 PARGETS *covers herself with cosmetics; the term was used of plastering or white-washing a wall.*

i'faith, Centaure. [*Exit Centaure.*] Good Sir Dauphine, solve it for
40   me. I'll call for it anon. [*Exit.*]

                [*Enter Clerimont.*]

    Clerimont. How now, Dauphine? How dost thou quit thyself of
these females?

    Dauphine. 'Slight, they haunt me like fairies, and give me jewels
here; I cannot be rid of 'em.

45   *Clerimont.* O, you must not tell, though.

    Dauphine. Mass, I forgot that; I was never so assaulted. One loves
for virtue, and bribes me with this. Another loves me with caution,
and so would possess me. A third brings me a riddle here, and all
are jealous and rail each at other.

50   *Clerimont.* A riddle? Pray' le' me see't?

                "Sir Dauphine,   *He reads the*
                                       paper.
I chose this way of intimation for privacy. The ladies here, I
know, have both hope and purpose to make a collegiate and servant
of you. If I might be so honored as to appear at any end of so noble
55   a work, I would enter into a fame of taking physic tomorrow and
continue it four or five days or longer, for your visitation. Mavis."

    By my faith, a subtle one! Call you this a riddle? What's their
plain dealing, trow?

    Dauphine. We lack Truewit to tell us that.

---

41 QUIT . . . OF *perhaps a quibble:* "*acquit yourself with*" *and* "*get rid of*".

45 TELL *to reveal a gift from the fairies would forfeit the gift and provoke the fairies'
   anger.*

46 MASS *mild oath:* "*by the Mass*".

47 THIS *Haughty's jewel.* ANOTHER *i.e., Centaure.*

55 ENTER . . . FAME *stilted way of saying,* "*start a rumor.*"
   TAKING PHYSIC *dosing with medicine, specifically a purge, and thus an excuse
   for staying home.*

56 VISITATION *i.e., of the sick, a charitable or pastoral duty.*

58 TROW *do you suppose? Cf. IV.5.34 and fn.*

Clerimont. We lack him for somewhat else too: his knights 60
reformados are wound up as high and insolent as ever they were.

Dauphine. You jest.

Clerimont. No drunkards, either with wine or vanity, ever confessed such stories of themselves. I would not give a fly's leg in balance against all the women's reputations here, if they could be but 65
thought to speak truth; and for the bride, they have made their
affidavit against her directly—

Dauphine. What, that they have lien with her?

Clerimont. Yes, and tell times and circumstances, with the cause
why and the place where. I had almost brought 'em to affirm that 70
they had done it today.

Dauphine. Not both of 'em.

Clerimont. Yes, faith; with a sooth or two more I had effected it.
They would ha' set it down under their hands.

Dauphine. Why, they will be our sport, I see, still, whether we 75
will or no.

61 REFORMADOS *reformed in military sense, officers of disbanded* ("*reformed*")
companies who retain rank and seniority.
68 LIEN *lain.*
73 SOOTH *flattery, blandishment.*

Act V Scene 3

[*Enter Truewit.*]

Truewit. O, are you here? Come, Dauphine. Go call your uncle
presently. I have fitted my divine and my canonist, dyed their beards

2 FITTED *furnished (i.e., dressed); generally, made ready.*
CANONIST *canon lawyer; see IV.4.131–32 and fn.*

and all. The knaves do not know themselves, they are so exalted and altered. Preferment changes any man. Thou shalt keep one door, and I another, and then Clerimont in the midst, that he may have no means of escape from their cavilling when they grow hot once. And then the women—as I have given the bride her instructions— to break in upon him i' the *l'envoy*. O, 'twill be full and twanging! Away, fetch him. [*Exit Dauphine; Otter and Cutbeard enter in their disguises.*] Come, Master Doctor and Master Parson, look to your parts now and discharge 'em bravely; you are well set forth, perform it as well. If you chance to be out, do not confess it with standing still or humming or gaping one at another, but go on and talk aloud and eagerly, use vehement action, and only remember your terms, and you are safe. Let the matter go where it will; you have many will do so. But at first, be very solemn, and grave like your garments, though you loose your selves after and skip out like a brace of jugglers on a table. Here he comes! Set your faces, and look superciliously while I present you.

[*Re-enter Dauphine with Morose.*]

Morose. Are these the two learned men?

Truewit. Yes, sir; please you salute 'em?

Morose. Salute 'em? I had rather do anything than wear out time so unfruitfully, sir. I wonder how these common forms, as "God save you" and "You are welcome," are come to be a habit in our

3 EXALTED *raised in rank; elated with pride.*

4–5 ONE . . . MIDST *the stages at Blackfriars and Whitefriars apparently had three doors, or a door on each side and a discovery space between.*

6 CAVILLING *raising frivolous objections.*

8 L'ENVOY *conclusion.*

TWANGING *lively.*

10 DOCTOR . . . PARSON *Cutbeard and Otter respectively.* N.

11 SET FORTH *equipped; dressed for the part.*

12 OUT *i.e., of things to say: disconcerted.*

15–16 YOU HAVE *i.e., there are.*

21 SALUTE *greet courteously.*

lives! or "I am glad to see you!" when I cannot see what the   25
profit can be of these words, so long as it is no whit better with
him whose affairs are sad and grievous, that he hears this salutation.

  Truewit. 'Tis true, sir; we'll go to the matter then. Gentlemen,
Master Doctor and Master Parson, I have acquainted you sufficiently
with the business for which you are come hither. And you are not   30
now to inform yourselves in the state of the question, I know. This
is the gentleman who expects your resolution, and therefore, when
you please, begin.

  Otter. Please, you, Master Doctor.

  Cutbeard. Please, you, good Master Parson.   35

  Otter. I would hear the canon law speak first.

  Cutbeard. It must give place to positive divinity, Sir.

  Morose. Nay, good gentlemen, do not throw me into circumstances. Let your comforts arrive quickly at me, those that are. Be
swift in affording me my peace, if so I shall hope any. I love not   40
your disputations or your court tumults. And that it be not strange
to you, I will tell you. My father, in my education, was wont to
advise me that I should always collect and contain my mind, not
suffering it to flow loosely; that I should look to what things were
necessary to the carriage of my life, and what not, embracing the one   45
and eschewing the other. In short, that I should endear myself to
rest and avoid turmoil, which now is grown to be another nature to
me. So that I come not to your public pleadings or your places of
noise; not that I neglect those things that make for the dignity of
the commonwealth, but for the mere avoiding of clamors, and   50
impertinencies of orators, that know not how to be silent. And for

30–31 YOU . . . QUESTION *you do not have to be told about this question.*
37 POSITIVE DIVINITY *practical, as opposed to speculative or theoretical theology.*
38–39 CIRCUMSTANCES *incidental or irrelevant details.*
43 COLLECT *control.*
51–52 FOR THE CAUSE OF *because of; perhaps in legal sense: Morose's "case" as*
    plaintiff.

the cause of noise am I now a suitor to you. You do not know in what a misery I have been exercised this day, what a torrent of evil! My very house turns round with the tumult! I dwell in a windmill!
55 The perpetual motion is here, and not at Eltham.

Truewit. Well, good Master Doctor, will you break the ice? Master Parson will wade after.

Cutbeard. Sir, though unworthy and the weaker, I will presume.

Otter. 'Tis no presumption, *domine* Doctor.

60 *Morose.* Yet again!

Cutbeard. Your question is, for how many causes a man may have *divortium legitimum*, a lawful divorce. First, you must understand the nature of the word divorce, *a divertendo*—

Morose. No excursions upon words, good Doctor; to the question
65 briefly.

Cutbeard. I answer then, the canon law affords divorce but in a few cases, and the principal is in the common case, the adulterous case. But there are *duodecim impedimenta*, twelve impediments—as we call 'em—all which do not *dirimere contractum*, but *irritum reddere*
70 *matrimonium*, as we say in the canon law, not take away the bond, but cause a nullity therein.

Morose. I understood you, before; good sir, avoid your impertinency of translation.

Otter. He cannot open this too much, sir, by your favor.

53 EXERCISED *tried, afflicted.*
55 PERPETUAL . . . ELTHAM *one of the sights of the time: a hollow glass globe supposedly capable of perpetual motion, built by Cornelius Drebbel, inventor patronized by James I, at Eltham, a village eight miles outside of London.*
59 DOMINE *master: used to address members of the clergy and learned professions.*
62 DIVORTIUM *N.*
63 A DIVERTENDO *from "separating."*
64 EXCURSIONS *digressions.*
66 CANON LAW *N.*
72–73 IMPERTINENCY *in literal and legal sense, irrelevance.*
74 OPEN *explain, interpret.*

Morose. Yet more! 75

Truewit. O, you must give the learned men leave, sir. To your impediments, Master Doctor.

Cutbeard. The first is *impedimentum erroris.*

Otter. Of which there are several species.

Cutbeard. Ay, as *error personæ.* 80

Otter. If you contract yourself to one person, thinking her another.

Cutbeard. Then, *error fortunae.*

Otter. If she be a beggar, and you thought her rich.

Cutbeard. Then, *error qualitatis.* 85

Otter. If she prove stubborn or headstrong, that you thought obedient.

Morose. How? Is that, sir, a lawful impediment? One at once, I pray you, gentlemen.

Otter. Ay, *ante copulam*, but not *post copulam*, sir. 90

Cutbeard. Master Parson says right. *Nec post nuptiarum benedictionem.* It doth indeed but *irrita reddere sponsalia*, annul the contract; after marriage it is of no obstancy.

Truewit. Alas, sir, what a hope are we fallen from, by this time!

Cutbeard. The next is *conditio*: if you thought her free born, and 95 she prove a bond-woman, there is impediment of estate and condition.

Otter. Ay, but Master Doctor, those servitudes are *sublatae* now, among us Christians.

88 ONE AT ONCE *i.e., give me a divorce on these grounds at once.*

90 COPULAM *technically, the legal and sacramental bond, not the physical union; but probably a play on both meanings.*

91–92 NEC . . . BENEDICTIONEM *and not after the marriage ceremony.*

93 OBSTANCY *legal opposition.*

94 TIME *timing.*

98 SERVITUDES ARE SUBLATAE *a little wild, as H & S points out: servitudes, strictly in law, refer to landed property, not personal relationships; sublatae means removed.*

100   *Cutbeard.* By your favor, Master Parson—

    Otter. You shall give me leave, Master Doctor.

    Morose. Nay, gentlemen, quarrel not in that question; it concerns not my case. Pass to the third.

    Cutbeard. Well, then, the third is *votum.* If either party have made
105 a vow of chastity. But that practice, as Master Parson said of the other, is taken away among us, thanks be to discipline. The fourth is *cognatio*: if the persons be of kin within the degrees.

    Otter. Ay. Do you know what the degrees are, sir?

    Morose. No, nor I care not, sir; they offer me no comfort in the
110 question, I am sure.

    Cutbeard. But there is a branch of this impediment may, which is *cognatio spiritualis.* If you were her god-father, sir, then the marriage is incestuous.

    Otter. That comment is absurd and superstitious, Master Doctor.
115 I cannot endure it. Are we not all brothers and sisters, and as much akin in that as god-fathers and god-daughters?

    Morose. O me! To end the controversy, I never was a god-father, I never was a god-father in my life, sir. Pass to the next.

    Cutbeard. The fifth is *crimen adulterii:* the known case. The sixth,
120 *cultus disparitas,* difference of religion. Have you ever examined her what religion she is of?

    Morose. No, I would rather she were of none than be put to the trouble of it!

    Otter. You may have it done for you, sir.

125   *Morose.* By no means, good sir; on to the rest. Shall you ever come to an end, think you?

---

106 DISCIPLINE *N.*

107 DEGREES *steps in direct line of descent within which marriage is prohibited.* Cognatio *refers to blood relationships.*

112–16 COGNATIO . . . GOD–DAUGHTERS *an instance of doctrinal difference between conservative (Cutbeard) and radical (Otter) clergy; see N. for l. 10.*

119 CRIMEN *either accusation or crime.*

Truewit. Yes, he has done half, sir.—On to the rest.—Be patient and expect, sir.

Cutbeard. The seventh is *vis*: if it were upon compulsion, or force.

Morose. O, no, it was too voluntary, mine—too voluntary. 130

Cutbeard. The eighth is *ordo*: if ever she have taken holy orders.

Otter. That's superstitious, too.

Morose. No matter, Master Parson. Would she would go into a nunnery yet.

Cutbeard. The ninth is *ligamen*: if you were bound, sir, to any other 135 before.

Morose. I thrust myself too soon into these fetters.

Cutbeard. The tenth is *publica honestas*, which is *inchoata quaedam affinitas.*

Otter. Ay, or *affinitas orta ex sponsalibus*, and is but *leve impedi-* 140 *mentum.*

Morose. I feel no air of comfort blowing to me, in all this.

Cutbeard. The eleventh is *affinitas ex fornicatione.*

Otter. Which is no less *vera affinitas* than the other, Master Doctor. 145

Cutbeard. True, *quae oritur ex legitimo matrimonio.*

Otter. You say right, venerable Doctor. And *nascitur ex eo, quod per conjugium duae personae efficiuntur una caro—*

Morose. Heyday, now they begin!

Cutbeard. I conceive you, Master Parson. *Ita per fornicationem* 150 *aeque est verus pater, qui sic generat—*

Otter. Et vere filius qui sic generatur—

---

128 EXPECT *wait (expectantly).*

138 PUBLICA HONESTAS *i.e., public notice of a marriage contract.*

138–39 INCHOATA . . . AFFINITAS *lit., "a certain incomplete relationship by marriage."*

140 AFFINITAS . . . SPONSALIBUS *relationship arising from a betrothal.*
  LEVE *light.*

143–52 AFFINITAS . . . GENERATUR *N.*

Morose. What's all this to me?

Clerimont. Now it grows warm.

155 *Cutbeard.* The twelfth and last is, *si forte coire nequibis.*

Otter. Ay, that is *impedimentum gravissimum.* It doth utterly annul and annihilate, that. If you have *manifestam frigiditatem*, you are well, sir.

Truewit. Why, there is comfort come at length, sir. Confess
160 yourself but a man unable, and she will sue to be divorced first.

Otter. Ay, or if there be *morbus perpetuus et insanabilis,* as paralysis, elephantiasis, or so—

Dauphine. O, but *frigiditas* is the fairer way, gentlemen.

Otter. You say troth, sir, and as it is in the canon, Master Doctor.

165 *Cutbeard.* I conceive you, sir.

Clerimont. Before he speaks.

Otter. That a boy, or child, under years, is not fit for marriage, because he cannot *reddere debitum.* So your *omnipotentes*—

Truewit. [*Aside to Otter.*] Your *impotentes*, you whoreson lobster.

170 *Otter.* Your *impotentes*, I should say, are *minime apti ad contrahenda matrimonium.*

Truewit. [*Aside to Otter.*] *Matrimonium?* We shall have most un-matrimonial Latin with you: *matrimonia*, and be hanged.

Dauphine. [*Aside to Truewit.*] You put 'em out, man.

175 *Cutbeard.* But then there will arise a doubt, Master Parson, in our case, *post matrimonium:* that *frigiditate praeditus*—do you conceive me, sir?

Otter. Very well, sir.

155 SI . . . NEQUIBUS *if one can copulate with no one; see N. for l. 66.*

161 MORBUS . . . INSANABILIS *a continual and incurable disease.*

168 REDDERE DEBITUM *render his debt.*

170–71 MINIME . . . MATRIMONIUM *least suited to contracting marriages.*

172 MATRIMONIUM *Otter's Latin slips a little, as Truewit points out; it should be plural to agree with contrahenda.*

174 PUT 'EM OUT *disconcert or upset them.*

176 PRAEDITUS *one who suffers from.*

Cutbeard. Who cannot *uti uxore pro uxore*, may *habere eam pro sorore.*   180

Otter. Absurd, absurd, absurd, and merely apostatical.

Cutbeard. You shall pardon me, Master Parson, I can prove it.

Otter. You can prove a will, Master Doctor, you can prove nothing else. Does not the verse of your own canon say, *Haec socianda vetant conubia, facta retractant—*   185

Cutbeard. I grant you, but how do they *retractare*, Master Parson?

Morose. O, this was it I feared.

Otter. In aeternum, sir.

Cutbeard. That's false in divinity, by your favor.

Otter. 'Tis false in humanity to say so. Is he not *prorsus inutilis ad*   190
thorum? Can he *praestare fidem datam*? I would fain know.

Cutbeard. Yes: how if he do *convalere*?

Otter. He cannot *convalere*, it is impossible.

Truewit. [*To Morose.*] Nay, good sir, attend the learned men; they'll think you neglect 'em else.   195

Cutbeard. Or if he do *simulare* himself *frigidum, odio uxoris*, or so?

Otter. I say he is *adulter manifestus* then.

Dauphine. They dispute it very learnedly, i'faith.

Otter. And *prostitutor uxoris*, and this is positive.

Morose. Good sir, let me escape.   200

179–80 UTI . . . SORORE *use a wife as a wife, may keep her as a sister.*

181 MERELY APOSTATICAL *absolutely heretical.*

183 PROVE A WILL *establish the validity of a will (Otter emphasizes Cutbeard's supposed knowledge of law, not of theology).*

184–85 HAEC . . . RETRACTANT *they forbid these marriages to be accomplished; they annul them, having been made. See N. for l. 66.*

190–91 PRORSUS . . . THORUM *utterly useless for the marriage bed.*

191 PRAESTARE . . . DATAM *discharge the word or promise that has been given.*

192 CONVALERE *get stronger.*

196 SIMULARE . . . UXORIS *pretend to be frigid, out of hatred for his wife.*

197 ADULTER MANIFESTUS *plain adulterer.*

199 PROSTITUTOR UXORIS *pander to his wife.*

     Truewit. You will not do me that wrong, sir?
     Otter. And therefore, if he be *manifeste frigidus*, sir—
     Cutbeard. Ay, if he be *manifeste frigidus*, I grant you—
     Otter. Why, that was my conclusion.
205   *Cutbeard.* And mine too.
     Truewit. Nay, hear the conclusion, sir.
     Otter. Then, *frigiditatis causa*—
     Cutbeard. Yes, *causa frigiditatis*—
     Morose. O, mine ears!
210   *Otter.* She may have *libellum divortii* against you.
     Cutbeard. Ay, *divortii libellum* she will sure have.
     Morose. Good echoes, forbear.
     Otter. If you confess it.
     Cutbeard. Which I would do, sir—
215   *Morose.* I will do anything—
     Otter. And clear myself *in foro conscientiae*—
     Cutbeard. Because you want indeed—
     Morose. Yet more?
     Otter. Exercendi potestate.

210 LIBELLUM DIVORTII *bill of divorce.*
216 IN FORO CONSCIENTIAE *at the bar of conscience.*
217 WANT *lack.*
219 EXERCENDI POTESTATE *the power of carrying out.*

Act V Scene 4

[*Enter Epicoene, Haughty, Centaure, Mavis, Mistress Otter, Daw, and
La Foole.*]
     Epicoene. I will not endure it any longer! Ladies, I beseech you
help me. This is such a wrong as never was offered to poor bride

before. Upon her marriage day, to have her husband conspire against her, and a couple of mercenary companions to be brought in for form's sake, to persuade a separation! If you had blood or virtue in you, gentlemen, you would not suffer such earwigs about a husband, or scorpions to creep between man and wife—

Morose. O the variety and changes of my torment!

Haughty. Let 'em be cudgelled out of doors by our grooms.

Centaure. I'll lend you my footman.

Mavis. We'll have our men blanket 'em i' the hall.

Mrs. Otter. As there was one at our house, madam, for peeping in at the door.

Daw. Content, i'faith.

Truewit. Stay, ladies and gentlemen, you'll hear before you proceed?

Mavis. I'd ha' the bridegroom blanketed too.

Centaure. Begin with him first.

Haughty. Yes, by my troth.

Morose. O mankind generation!

Dauphine. Ladies, for my sake forbear.

Haughty. Yes, for Sir Dauphine's sake.

Centaure. He shall command us.

La Foole. He is as fine a gentleman of his inches, madam, as any is about the town, and wears as good colors when he list.

Truewit. Be brief, sir, and confess your infirmity, she'll be a-fire to be quit of you; if she but hear that named once, you shall not

4 COMPANIONS *used contemptuously: confederates.*

6 EARWIGS *insects, so-called because they were thought to penetrate into the head through the ear; see l. 216 and fn.*

11 BLANKET *toss in a blanket.*

20 MANKIND *savage, dangerous to men; also, unnaturally masculine. N.*

24 OF HIS INCHES *of his stature.*

25 COLORS *heraldic colors or the insignia of a knight.*

entreat her to stay. She'll fly you like one that had the marks upon him.

30   *Morose.* Ladies, I must crave all your pardons—

Truewit. Silence, ladies.

Morose. For a wrong I have done to your whole sex in marrying this fair and virtuous gentlewoman—

Clerimont. Hear him, good ladies.

35   *Morose.* Being guilty of an infirmity which, before I conferred with these learned men, I thought I might have concealed—

Truewit. But now being better informed in his conscience by them, he is to declare it, and give satisfaction by asking your public forgiveness.

40   *Morose.* I am no man, ladies.

All. How!

Morose. Utterly unabled in nature, by reason of frigidity, to perform the duties or any the least office of a husband.

Mavis. Now, out upon him, prodigious creature!

45   *Centaure.* Bridegroom uncarnate.

Haughty. And would you offer it, to a young gentlewoman?

Mrs. Otter. A lady of her longings?

Epicoene. Tut, a device, a device, this, it smells rankly, ladies. A mere comment of his own.

50   *Truewit.* Why, if you suspect that, ladies, you may have him searched.

Daw. As the custom is, by a jury of physicians.

La Foole. Yes, faith, 'twill be brave.

28 MARKS *of the plague? or pox?*

45 UNCARNATE *without a body.*

46 OFFER IT *a characteristic collegiate ambiguity: "offer" may mean 1. propose, 2. present, proffer, 3. attempt; the antecedent of "it" thus may be 1. marriage, 2. the "uncarnate" condition, 3. deception, insult.*

49 COMMENT *(Latin* commentum *= falsehood) sometimes a "lie or fayned tale"* (*J. Bullokar*, An English Expositor, *1616*).

53 BRAVE *splendid.*

Morose. O me, must I undergo that!

Mrs. Otter. No, let women search him, madam: we can do it   55
ourselves.

Morose. Out on me, worse!

Epicoene. No, ladies, you shall not need, I'll take him with all his
faults.

Morose. Worst of all!   60

Clerimont. Why, then 'tis no divorce, Doctor, if she consent not?

Cutbeard. No, if the man be *frigidus*, it is *de parte uxoris* that we
grant *libellum divortii*, in the law.

Otter. Ay, it is the same in theology.

Morose. Worse, worse than worst!   65

Truewit. Nay, sir, be not utterly disheartened, we have yet a small
relic of hope left, as near as our comfort is blown out. Clerimont,
produce your brace of knights. What was that, Master Parson, you
told me *in errore qualitatis*, e'en now? [*Aside.*] Dauphine, whisper
the bride that she carry it as if she were guilty and ashamed.   70

Otter. Marry, sir, *in errore qualitatis*—which Master Doctor did forbear to urge—if she be found *corrupta*, that is, vitiated or broken up,
that was *pro virgine desponsa*, espoused for a maid—

Morose. What then, sir?

Otter. It doth *dirimere contractum* and *irritum reddere* too.   75

Truewit. If this be true, we are happy again, sir, once more. Here
are an honorable brace of knights that shall affirm so much.

Daw. Pardon us, good Master Clerimont.

La Foole. You shall excuse us, Master Clerimont.

Clerimont. Nay, you must make it good now, knights, there is no   80
remedy; I'll eat no words for you nor no men. You know you
spoke it to me?

72 VITIATED . . . UP *deflowered. Presumably Otter distinguishes between enticement
to vice and forcible rape.*

75 DIRIMERE . . . REDDERE *dissolve the contract and render it null and void.*

Daw. Is this gentleman-like, sir?

Truewit. [*Aside to Daw.*] Jack Daw, he's worse than Sir Amorous,
85 fiercer a great deal. [*Aside to La Foole.*] Sir Amorous, beware, there be
ten Daws in this Clerimont.

La Foole. I'll confess it, sir.

Daw. Will you, Sir Amorous? Will you wound reputation?

La Foole. I am resolved.

90 *Truewit.* So should you be too, Jack Daw. What should keep
you off? She is but a woman, and in disgrace. He'll be glad on 't.

Daw. Will he? I thought he would ha' been angry.

Clerimont. You will dispatch, knights; it must be done, i'faith.

Truewit. Why, an' it must, it shall, sir, they say. They'll ne'er go
95 back. [*Aside to them.*] Do not tempt his patience.

Daw. It is true indeed, sir.

La Foole. Yes, I assure you, sir.

Morose. What is true, gentlemen? What do you assure me?

Daw. That we have known your bride, sir—

100 *La Foole.* In good fashion. She was our mistress, or so—

Clerimont. Nay, you must be plain, knights, as you were to me.

Otter. Ay, the question is, if you have *carnaliter* or no.

La Foole. *Carnaliter*? What else, sir?

Otter. It is enough: a plain nullity.

105 *Epicoene.* I am undone, I am undone!

Morose. O, let me worship and adore you, gentlemen!

Epicoene. [*Weeping.*] I am undone!

Morose. Yes, to my hand, I thank these knights. Master Parson,
let me thank you otherwise. [*Gives him money.*]

110 *Centaure.* And ha' they confessed?

Mavis. Now out upon 'em, informers!

84 HE'S *Clerimont.*
99 KNOWN *had sexual intercourse with.*
108 TO MY HAND *into my power. See IV.5.15 and fn.*

Truewit. You see what creatures you may bestow your favors on, madams.

Haughty. I would except against 'em as beaten knights, wench, and not good witnesses in law.   115

Mrs. Otter. Poor gentlewoman, how she takes it!

Haughty. Be comforted, Morose, I love you the better for't.

Centaure. So do I, I protest.

Cutbeard. But, gentlemen, you have not known her since *matrimonium*?   120

Daw. Not today, Master Doctor.

La Foole. No, sir, not today.

Cutbeard. Why, then I say, for any act before, the *matrimonium* is good and perfect, unless the worshipful bridegroom did precisely, before witness, demand if she were *virgo ante nuptias*.   125

Epicoene. No, that he did not, I assure you, Master Doctor.

Cutbeard. If he cannot prove that, it is *ratum conjugium*, notwithstanding the premises. And they do no way *impedire*. And this is my sentence, this I pronounce.

Otter. I am of Master Doctor's resolution too, sir: if you made   130
not that demand *ante nuptias*.

Morose. O my heart! Wilt thou break? Wilt thou break? This is worst of all worst worsts that hell could have devised! Marry a whore! And so much noise!

Dauphine. Come, I see now plain confederacy in this Doctor and   135
this Parson to abuse a gentleman. You study his affliction. I pray be gone, companions. And gentlemen, I begin to suspect you for having parts with 'em. Sir, will it please you hear me?

114–15 EXCEPT . . . LAW *object to their testimony as inadmissible, on the grounds that knights proven to be cowardly are presumed forsworn, and therefore cannot serve on a jury or be admitted as witnesses in any case at law (from Gifford, as quoted in H & S).*

127 RATUM *ratified; legal.*

136 STUDY *scrutinize (in order to exploit).*

138 HAVING PARTS *sharing or cooperating.*

167

Morose. O, do not talk to me, take not from me the pleasure of
140 dying in silence, nephew.

Dauphine. Sir, I must speak to you. I have been long your poor
despised kinsman, and many a hard thought has strengthened you
against me; but now it shall appear if either I love you or your peace,
and prefer them to all the world beside. I will not be long or grievous
145 to you, sir. If I free you of this unhappy match absolutely and instantly, after all this trouble, and almost in your despair now—

Morose. It cannot be—

Dauphine. Sir, that you be never troubled with a murmur of it
more, what shall I hope for or deserve of you?

150 *Morose.* O, what thou wilt, nephew! Thou shalt deserve me and
have me.

Dauphine. Shall I have your favor perfect to me, and love
hereafter?

Morose. That and anything beside. Make thine own conditions.
155 My whole estate is thine. Manage it, I will become thy ward.

Dauphine. Nay, sir, I will not be so unreasonable.

Epicoene. Will Sir Dauphine be mine enemy too?

Dauphine. You know I have been long a suitor to you, uncle, that
out of your estate, which is fifteen hundred a year, you would
160 allow me but five hundred during life, and assure the rest upon me
after, to which I have often by myself and friends tendered you a
writing to sign, which you would never consent or incline to. If you
please but to effect it now—

Morose. Thou shalt have it, nephew. I will do it, and more.

165 *Dauphine.* If I quit you not presently and forever of this cumber,
you shall have power instantly, afore all these, to revoke your act,
and I will become whose slave you will give me to forever.

162 to] F₂; too F₁.

———

165 CUMBER *burden, distress.*

168

Morose. Where is the writing? I will seal to it, that, or to a blank, and write thine own conditions.

Epicoene. O me, most unfortunate, wretched gentlewoman! 170

Haughty. Will Sir Dauphine do this?

Epicoene. Good sir, have some compassion on me.

Morose. O, my nephew knows you belike; away, crocodile!

Centaure. He does it not, sure, without good ground.

Dauphine. Here, sir. [*Gives him the papers.*] 175

Morose. Come, nephew, give me the pen. I will subscribe to anything, and seal to what thou wilt, for my deliver- [*Signing the papers.*] ance. Thou art my restorer. Here, I deliver it thee as my deed. If there be a word in it lacking, or writ with false orthography, I protest before God I will not take the advantage. 180

Dauphine. Then here is your release, sir; you have *He takes off* married a boy: a gentleman's son that I have brought *Epicoene's peruke.* up this half year at my great charges, and for this composition which I have now made with you. What say you, Master Doctor? This is *justum impedimentum*, I hope, *error personae*? 185

Otter. Yes, sir, *in primo gradu*.

Cutbeard. *In primo gradu.*

Dauphine. I thank you, good Doctor Cutbeard and Parson Otter. You are beholden to 'em, sir, that have taken this pains *He pulls off their beards, and* for you, and my friend, Master Truewit, who enabled *disguise.* 190 'em for the business. Now you may go in and rest, be as private as you will, sir. I'll not trouble you till you trouble me with your funeral, which I care not how soon it come. [*Exit Morose.*] Cut-

---

180 before God] before—F. See fn.

---

173 BELIKE *probably, in all likelihood.*

    CROCODILE *reputed to shed tears over its prey before devouring it.*

180 BEFORE GOD *in the context one would expect "before God," as H & S indicate.*

183 COMPOSITION *contract; arrangement involving surrender or sacrifice on one side or both.*

beard, I'll make your lease good. Thank me not but with your leg,
195 Cutbeard. And Tom Otter, your Princess shall be reconciled to
you. How now, gentlemen! Do you look at me?

Clerimont. A boy!

Dauphine. Yes, Mistress Epicoene.

Truewit. Well, Dauphine, you have lurched your friends of the
200 better half of the garland, by concealing this part of the plot! But
much good do it thee, thou deserv'st it, lad. And Clerimont, for
thy unexpected bringing in these two to confession, wear my part
of it freely. Nay, Sir Daw and Sir La Foole, you see the gentlewoman
that has done you the favors! We are all thankful to you, and so
205 should the womankind here, specially for lying on her, though not
with her! You meant so, I am sure? But that we have stuck it upon
you today in your own imagined persons, and so lately, this
Amazon, the champion of the sex, should beat you now thriftily for
the common slanders which ladies receive from such cuckoos as you
210 are. You are they that, when no merit or fortune can make you
hope to enjoy their bodies, will yet lie with their reputations and
make their fame suffer. Away, you common moths of these and all
ladies' honors. Go, travel to make legs and faces, and come home
with some new matter to be laughed at: you deserve to live in an
215 air as corrupted as that wherewith you feed rumor. [*Exeunt Daw and
La Foole.*] Madams, you are mute upon this new metamorphosis!

213 travel] travaile F. See fn.

194 MAKE . . . GOOD "*give thee the lease of thy house free*" (II.5.81–82).
199 LURCHED *robbed, cheated* (*OED*).
205 ON *about.*
206–07 BUT . . . YOU *if we had not fastened the lie on to you.*
209 CUCKOOS *fools; also as birds who lay their eggs in the nests of other birds.
See next sentence.*
213 TRAVEL *contemporary rhymes indicate no difference in pronunciation, but the
F. spelling indicates a meaning we could express only as a pun.*
TRAVEL . . . FACES *travel to learn how to bow and simper.*

But here stands she that has vindicated your fames. Take heed of such *insectae* hereafter. And let it not trouble you that you have discovered any mysteries to this young gentleman. He is, a'most, of years, and will make a good visitant within this twelvemonth. In the 220 meantime we'll all undertake for his secrecy, that can speak so well of his silence. [*Coming forward.*] Spectators, if you like this comedy, rise cheerfully, and now Morose is gone in, clap your hands. It may be that noise will cure him, at least please him. [*Exeunt.*]

218 INSECTAE *as H & S point out, the correct Latin plural is neuter,* insecta; *the OED credits Jonson with being the first to make the mistake of treating it as feminine, but in the context it is not inconceivable that Jonson, or Truewit, deliberately blunders.*

219–20 OF YEARS *mature.*

THE END.

Notes

SIR FRANCIS STUART *Second son of James Stewart and Elizabeth, Countess of Moray; through his maternal grandfather, the regent of Scotland, who was the illegitimate son of James V, he could claim descent from the older sister of Henry VIII, Margaret of England, wife of James IV of Scotland, with whom the Stuart succession originates. He was created a Knight of the Bath in June of 1610, a few months after Jonson's play was first presented, and was influential both at court and in London literary circles. Aubrey refers to him as a "learned Gentleman, and one of the Club at the Mermaid, in Fryday street, with Sir Walter Ralegh, etc., of that Sodalitie: Heroes and Witts of that time."* [1]

5 DISPLEASED NONE *Here and in the second prologue Jonson alludes to the trouble which the play caused him. See the Appendix, p. 200.*

THE PERSONS OF THE PLAY

By using a character's name to emphasize a salient trait, Jonson often suggests how we are to see and judge that character. "Morose," borrowed with part of the plot from a story by the Greek rhetorician, Libanius, echoes the Latin morosus: *excessively addicted to a habit* (mos, moris). *To the Jacobeans "morose" implied a crossness rather than the damp sadness we now associate with it.* [2] *"Dauphine"*

---

1. *Aubrey's Brief Lives*, ed. O. L. Dick (London, 1949), p. cx.
2. See Randle Cotgrave, *A Dictionarie of the French and English Tongues* (London, 1632), "morositie" and "*morosité*"; and John Bullokar, *An English Expositor* (London, 1616), "morositie."

was then as well as later the title of the heir apparent of the King of France, hence an appropriate comic hyperbole for Morose's heir. "Eugenie" brings out his noble nature and, perhaps, as Otto Hinze claims, his intelligent mind through the French génie, wit.[3] The name of "Clerimont," that defender of simplicity and naturalness in dress and make-up, may echo the French clairement, *clearly, plainly, brightly, though it may serve too as tonal coloring. "Truewit" ought to suggest more of the Elizabethan wit than of the modern—more of ingenious inventiveness than of sophisticated repartee. "Epicoene" means adapted to both sexes. Certain names diminish their bearers by placing them in the animal world. The surname "Daw" degrades Sir John to the level of a stupid bird often tamed and noted for stealing small articles. Both "Centaure" and "Otter" suggest the sexual ambiguity of the women. The Renaissance had inherited the centaur, a half-horse, half-man, from the Greeks. The Elizabethans were so uncertain about the otter that they could not decide whether it was flesh or fish, and even thought that both sexes of the Ichneumon (a mongoose which they considered a kind of otter) bore young, "having seed in themselves, whereby they conceive."[4] The best gloss on "Mavis" appears in Florio's Italian dictionary (1611):* maviso, *for* malviso, *an ill face. Note Centaure's remark that Mavis has "a worse face" than Haughty (V.2.32).*

PROLOGUE

2 TO CONTENT THE PEOPLE *An echo of the opening lines of the prologue to Terence's* Andria (*which Jonson refers to in* The Magnetic Lady, Induction, *41–47), especially of* "populo ut placerent quas fecisset fabulas." *Compare with the Horatian doctrine of* "profit and delight" *in the next prologue.*

4 SECT OF WRITERS *No editor speculates on what group Jonson had in mind. He may be referring to such authors of sensational plays as Marston, Tourneur, and Middleton, or even to Chapman, who professed to hate the "prophane multitude."*

9 COOK'S TASTES *The play on taste is traditional in criticism from classical Latin on. See Martial, IX.81.3–4.*

---

3. Hinze, *Studien zu Ben Jonsons Namengebung in seinen Dramen* (Leipzig, 1919), p. 43. Robert Knoll is particularly helpful on the names: *Ben Jonson's Plays* (Lincoln, Nebraska, 1964), pp. 106–17.

4. Edward Topsell, *The Historie of Foure-footed beastes . . .* (London, 1607), pp. 448–49. He does not repeat this horrifying notion when he describes the otter itself (pp. 572–75).

22–24 BE FIT FOR LADIES . . . WHITEFRIARS *This reference to the different tastes of the audience was a commonplace in the Renaissance—and has been since. It appears in modern criticism in T. S. Eliot's claim that "several levels of significance" appear in Shakespeare's plays and that different levels appeal to different auditors—for some, the plot; for others, character, or rhythm, or diction.[5] Jonson's explicit separation of himself from the "sect of writers" who care only for "particular likings" suggests that he did not want to confine his audience to too narrow a group.*

24 WHITEFRIARS *Both a somewhat disreputable precinct of the city and a group of buildings, the former priory of the Carmelites, which lay between Fleet Street and the Thames. Epicoene was first produced in the hall of these buildings, a rectangular, roofed structure, with benches for sitting, candles and torches for lighting, and probably some scenery. Since this Whitefriars theater was enclosed, heated, and lit, it could be used winter and summer, night and day. Because it was expensive (between sixpence and one shilling), it was regularly patronized only by those who could afford it: that is, the gentry, barristers from the Inns of Court, and the rich.*

Act I, Scene 1

20 RUSHES *Since fresh rushes were strewn for visitors, Clerimont is alluding to the Boy's future warm welcome by the lady who now is cold to his master.*

47 TIME *Truewit continues here his ironic expression of the evanescence of time which haunts this play. Gentlemen melt away their time, gambling, visiting, eating, drinking, courting, and kissing, and never thinking of tomorrow until they have no tomorrow to think of. Truewit claims that he enters into some transient pleasures only "for company"—but he does enter and thus mocks himself out of time as skillfully and subtly as any other gentleman who avoids thinking of last things by concerning himself with present things.*

49 FINELIEST *Only Truewit uses the inflected form of adverbs ending in –ly (see also II.2.84), which had been displaced by the periphrastic comparison ("most finely") in cultivated speech.[6] This old-fashioned form may be Jonson's way of calling attention to Truewit's elaborate language.*

5. Eliot, *The Use of Poetry and the Use of Criticism* (Cambridge, Mass., 1933), p. 146.

6. A. C. Partridge, *The Accidence of Ben Jonson's Plays, Masques, and Entertainments* (Cambridge, 1953), pp. 135–36. See also W. Franz, *Shakespeare-Grammatik* (Heidelberg, 1924), sect. 246.

69–73 COLLEGIATES . . . AUTHORITY *These ladies aspire to be courtly, but Clerimont, who has just come from court, has not heard of them. They comprise an order between those who frequent the court and those who are still countrified. While living away from their husbands, they entertain fashionable cliques of the witty and the well-dressed, and judge, with most unfeminine decisiveness, the achievements of both the Wits and the Braveries (that is, a "brain" or a "fashion"). Later, both qualities will unite in the Restoration man of mode—a Dorimant or a Mirabell who combines real elegance with true wit. In this play we have gentlemen who possess wit, but no elegance (Morose), a little elegance but no wit (La Foole), neither (Daw), and both (Dauphine). Jonson covers the whole spectrum of modishness in men, but portrays only deviant women.*

79–113 SCOURED . . . FINISHED *Throughout this passage Jonson creates his special indecorum. "Scour" (l. 79) meant then as now to cleanse metal or wood by hard rubbing with a detergent. Applied to a woman's face and body, it prepares us to see her as the statuary she becomes in ll. 110–11. Observe too how the verb "put on" in l. 106 governs all the objects in its sentence. To put on a peruke is one thing; to put on eyebrows and fingernails quite another. H & S cite this as the first of many adaptations from Ovid's* Ars Amatoria, *III.135–40. Pope in* The Rape Of The Lock *borrows the wit in "repair" and "mend" and "sacred."*

82–93 SONG *A demonstration of the art Jonson called "Imitation" in his list of the qualifications required of the poet: "to bee able to convert the substance, or Riches of an other* Poet, *to his owne use" (H & S, 8:638). Clerimont's song converts the substance of a poem found in a Leyden manuscript of the* Anthologia Latina (*Codex Vossianus, Q. 86); it had been published by Scaliger in 1572, and versions of it were appended to late sixteenth-century editions of the* Satyricon *of Petronius (H & S, where the poem is quoted in full and later "imitations" are noted). Jonson makes elaborate use of the more familiar riches of Ovid and Juvenal; see the preceding note, and II.2.14–15 ff., IV.1.29 ff.*

110–13 ALDGATE . . . FINISHED *This passage shows how Jonson often worked with metaphor. To illustrate the value of concealed cosmetic artistry, he draws on both Ovid and a concrete London sight familiar to most of his audience—the tearing down and rebuilding of Aldgate, the principal eastern gate of the old city. The Ovidian advice fused with a topical image of statuary creates the peculiar effect that Jonson at his best can consummately achieve: an image vivid, extravagant, comically indecorous. Women, for the frozen moment of their perfection, become monuments, no longer rude, but painted, burnished, and finished. Anthony Munday, who edited and added to* The Survay of London *first written by John Stow, describes the gate as Jonson's audience might have seen it when it was being built in 1609–10: "to grace each side of the Gate, are set two Feminine personages, the one South-ward appearing to be Peace, with a siluer Doue upon her one hand, and a guilded wreath or Garland in the other. On the North side standeth Charity, with a child at her brest, and another led in her hand. Implying (as I conceive) that where Peace, and Loue or Charity do prosper, and are truely embraced, that Citie shall be for euer blessed."* 7

135–36 FISH-WIVES *Notoriously, fishwives and orange-women hawk their wares with piercing voices. Jonson describes in this passage the various sounds which made London so noisy, and so unbearable for a hypochondriac like Morose.*

146 WAITS *"A small body of wind instrumentalists maintained . . . at the public charge" to play on holidays or other special occasions, sometimes as they walked the city streets, at night or early in the morning (OED).*

163–66 BELLS . . . SICKNESS *Since the London of 1609 was a city of 114 churches, it was even on a normal day pleasingly full of chiming and ringing. A German visitor, Paul Hentzner, noticed in the 1590s that the English were "vastly fond of great noises that fill the ear, such as the firing of cannon, drums, and the ringing of bells, so that in London it is common for a number of them, that have got a glass in their heads, to go up into some belfry, and ring the bells for hours together, for the sake of exercise."* 8 *For a man who in Queen Elizabeth's time absented himself on weekends and holy days solely to avoid church bells, the "perpetuity of ringing" from the "passing" bells tolling the death knell during the plague must have been an acute discomfort.*

Act I, Scene 2

32–33 WOMAN . . . BARBER *The comic peripeteia of the whole plot is emphasized by Truewit's remark: "A woman, and a barber, and love no noise!" Any man who hates noise seals his loud fate by making a barber "chief of his counsel" and by taking a wife—women and barbers being the very archetypes of loquacity.*

7. Stow, *The Survay of London*, continued by A. Munday (London, 1618), p. 231.

8. Hentzner, *A Journey into England in the Year M.D.XC.VIII* (1757), p. 89.

45 IN CONSCIENCE *As a joke, Truewit adopts a cynical stance which is assumed more maliciously by Joseph Surface in Sheridan's* School For Scandal. *Any man low enough to suspect another without cause deserves the suffering he receives when given just cause for his suspicions. As Truewit says earlier (ll. 11–12), Morose's intention to disinherit Dauphine authorizes them to plague him. In thus asserting his moral obligation to torment so disagreeable a person as Morose, Truewit makes an apologia for ridiculing fools which is similar to the apologia of the satirical poets, including Jonson. We must distinguish, of course, between asserting one's right to the comic by writing a play and asserting such a right by playing a trick. Indeed, throughout* Epicoene *we must make a number of discriminations about trickery. For instance, Truewit's trickery, which gives him no more profit than the pleasurable exercise of his wit, involves little of the selfishness that necessarily belongs to the actions of Morose and Dauphine, both of whom have specific material rewards in mind.*

Act I, Scene 3

50 BREATH *The effeminacy of Sir Amorous is suggested by Clerimont's description of his speech. Instead of speaking in the measured periods of the grave gentleman or with the sprightly variety of a young man-about-town like Truewit, Sir Amorous speaks rapidly and spasmodically, gasping for air and gushing forth with imperfectly accented phrases. The prime example of such speech occurs in I.4.34–59. Note Clerimont's comment in I.4.69.*

Act I, Scene 4

10–12 WAIT UPON . . . DISPENSE *This passage contains two characteristic examples of how Jonson used the multiple meanings of words for comic effect. "Wait upon" could mean: pay a respectful visit to; attend as a servant; accompany, escort. Sir Amorous uses it in the last sense, but Clerimont mocks this hapless phrase by taking it in the second sense given above. The answer of Sir Amorous involves him in another semantic confusion. "Dispense with" could mean: do away with, put up with the absence of, excuse, deal with indulgently. Sir Amorous apparently means it in the last or even the next to the last sense. But Clerimont's "O, that I will" probably alludes to the first two meanings, neither of which Sir Amorous is quick enough to understand. Here the ability of a character to distinguish between different senses of words is an index of both manners and intelligence.*

52 KNIGHTED *The audience of 1609–10 might well have remembered the notorious*

Irish knighthoods created only ten years before by the Earl of Essex, who cheapened the honor through overuse. The absurdity of Sir Amorous's tarnished title is increased by his confused syntax, which allows one to conclude that he got his knighthood when he was a page to Lady Lofty's gentleman usher—but only after his elder brother died.

55 ISLAND VOYAGE *La Foole condemns himself by his allusion to the Island Voyage of 1597, the unsuccessful expedition led by Essex, Howard, and Raleigh against the Spanish in the Azores. In his superb description of this attack, one of the English captains, Sir Arthur Gorges, severely criticized the fashionable gallants who deserted at Plymouth, their courage cooled by a violent storm; he found especially reprehensible their delicate dress: they came to war "rather like Maskers then Souldiers." See* Purchas His Pilgrimes, *IV.x.1938–69.*

Act II, Scene 1

1 SD MUTE *The term seems to apply only loosely to the servant here, since he is not really or consistently mute in any sense. But Morose's insistence that his servant be a mute suggests that the term may be employed almost in a punning sense, as a kind of theatrical joke. If the term appeared only in scene headings or stage directions, the punning effect would be confined to a reading of the play, but when Truewit exits saying, "Farewell, Mute" (II.2.125), he brings the double meaning into the actual performance.*

26–33 TURK . . . FELICITY *Richard Knolles'* Generall Historie of the Turkes *(1603) is customarily thought to have set the Jacobean stereotype of "the glorious Empire of the Turkes, the present terrour of the world." Mutes, for instance, are described by Knolles as "strong men bereft of their speech, whom the Turkish tyrants have alwaies in readinesse, the more secretly to execute their bloody butchery."* [9] *For his knowledge of life at the Ottoman court Knolles drew heavily on the letters of Ogier Ghiselin de Busbecq, who was Charles the Fifth's ambassador to the court of Suleiman the Magnificent in 1555. Busbecq's first view of the Sultan's court may be the basis of Morose's rhapsody on the "divine discipline" of unquestioning obedience: "I was greatly struck with the silence and order that prevailed in this great crowd. There were no cries, no hum of voices, the usual accompaniments of a motley gathering, neither was there any jostling; without the slightest disturbance each man took his proper place*

---

9. *Generall Historie,* 5th ed. (1638), p. 763.

according to his rank."[10] *He was later even more impressed by the profound silence and order maintained by a multitude of soldiers and court officials during the celebration of a religious rite on a plain before the tents of the Sultan: " The men were so motionless that they seemed rooted to the ground on which they stood. There was no coughing, no clearing of the throat, and no voice to be heard, and no one looked behind him or moved his head."*[11] Samuel C. Chew's The Crescent and the Rose: Islam and England During the Renaissance (*1937*) *surveys the literary effects of such stereotypes of Islam (see pp. 139–41, 164–68, 493–96, 553–54).*

Act II, Scene 2

4 HARPOCRATES *The Greek name for the Egyptian sun god, Horus, who was often represented as a boy holding a finger on his mouth, and hence mistakenly considered the god of silence. Sometimes in Greek literature he was identified with Heracles, from whom he apparently acquired his club.*

14–15 THEY . . . MARRY *Truewit's diatribe against wives, which takes up the rest of the scene, is carefully and extensively modeled on the* Sixth Satire *of Juvenal. It is a fine example of how Jonson borrows another poet's riches for his own use. The details of the Roman poem are transposed into the context of contemporary London life with Augustan wit and ingenuity. The result is to torment Morose, to flood his elaborate artifice with a torrent of speech that proclaims itself in the same breath as both life and the most artful literature. In "Ovid, Juvenal, and 'The Silent Woman,'"* PMLA, *71 (March, 1956), 213–24, Jonas Barish comments perceptively on this passage. He is especially convincing when he claims that Truewit carries the manner of Juvenal to such outrageous lengths that his attitude emerges as a parody of Juvenal and the satiric outlook in general. See the introduction for further comments on Jonson's ironic attitude toward the young gentlemen.*

96 STATESWOMAN *A satiric coinage for a then-rare woman—one who took part in the conduct of public affairs. Note the affairs she conducts: news of the races held at Salisbury, goings-on at Bath (then fashionable only for bathing in its springs), court, or the King's progresses.*

---

10. *The Life and Letters of Ogier Ghiselin de Busbecq*, trans. C. T. Forster and F. H. B. Daniell (London, 1881), 1:156.

11. Ibid., p. 303.

98–99 DANIEL . . . YOUTH *Samuel Daniel and Edmund Spenser were sometimes compared by contemporaries (understandably on the basis of their sonnet sequences,* Delia *and* Amoretti; *inexplicably on the basis of their longer works—Daniel's epic,* Civil Wars Between Lancaster and York, *scarcely belongs to the same world as the* Faerie Queene). *No one knows who "tother youth" is meant to be. H & S suggest Daniel on no discernible evidence except perhaps Jonson's contempt for his versifying. John Upton suggests Thomas Dekker, apparently because of Jonson's attack on him in* Poetaster. *Gifford thinks Marston a more likely choice.*[12]

116 RISES *Cunningham (3: 516), thinks "rises" may be a misprint for "rinses," but both the Folio and the Quarto have "rises"—which is funnier than "rinses."*

118–19 CONVEYANCE *Legally, the transference of property by any lawful act. Jonson often uses financial terms in referring to sex and marriage for ironic effect, juxtaposing virginity and property, sexual experience and an estate, seducing an engaged woman and antedating a legal document.*

Act II, Scene 3

40–41 SENECA . . . PLUTARCH *Dauphine and Clerimont ironically emphasize the inanity of Daw's poem by pretending that it resembles the writing of either Seneca or Plutarch. The son of Seneca the Rhetorician, Seneca "the Younger" (ca. 4 B.C.–A.D. 65) was a Roman Stoic, essayist, and playwright, whose plays Daw scoffs at in l. 68, apparently without understanding that "Seneca the tragedian" is the same as Seneca the essayist. Plutarch (A.D. 45–120) was known in the Renaissance as much for his essays,* Moralia *(see I.1.62), as for his* Lives. *The highly-reputed essays of both were so often cited as mines of moral wisdom that Daw's attack on them points up his sententiousness and pretentious stupidity. Part of the jest lies also in the suggestion that the poem is prosaic enough to be mistaken for a prose essay.*

54–60 ARISTOTLE . . . HORACE *Someone seems to be playing learned word games here—perhaps Daw, perhaps Jonson at Daw's expense. The quibbles are typical of the tiresome academic jokes circulated during the Renaissance. Is Aristotle both "commonplace" (trite and unoriginal) and the great philosopher of the "common place" (Latin* locus communis), *a general theme applicable to many particular cases? Is Plato a "discourser" because he wrote dialogues, as well as*

---

12. John Upton, *Remarks on Three Plays of Benjamin Jonson* (London, 1749), p. 70. Gifford, 3:360.

because his dialogues best illustrate discourse, defined by Johnson as "the act of understanding, by which it passes from premises to consequences"? Are we supposed to hear "tedious" in the final syllables of Thucydides? Is Livy "dry" because livid (from Latin liveo), *or black and blue, is the color of the melancholy (that is, the absolutely dry) humor? Is Tacitus a "knot" because Latin* tacitus *means silent and concealed? The references to the poets may reflect bad reading on Daw's part rather than strained academic humor. To him Homer appears more as a writer on animal husbandry than as an epic poet, perhaps because of the numerous horses in the* Iliad *(such as the speaking horse in* XIX, *the chariot races in* XXIII, *and, of course, the Trojan Horse). The "chines of beef" probably refers, as* H & S *points out, to the Iliad,* VII.321. *Daw knows only the Vergil of the* Georgics *and not even the* Ars Poetica *of Horace, one of the most influential works of literary criticism in the Renaissance.*

59–60 CURRIERS . . . BEES *Daw's syntax involves him in an unintended quibble on currying horses (that is, dressing them with a comb) and currying food (because of the following reference to "chines of beef"). Another kind of syntactic trouble appears in the reference to "dunging of land, and bees," a phrase which allows one to consider cross-pollination and the making of honey in a new and ridiculous light.*

62–64 PINDARUS . . . FLACCUS *Daw demonstrates his ignorance when he tries to show off his learning. The comments by Dauphine and Clerimont enable us to judge the scene: "What a sackful of their names he has got!" He has acquired their names without understanding their works. Furthermore, as Dauphine points out, his serial name-dropping lacks any discrimination. For example, he puts Politian or Angelo Poliziano, the fifteenth-century humanist, next to Valerius Flaccus, the Roman poet* (A.D. 70–79) *who wrote the* Argonautica. *Most of the authors in his first sackful are too well-known to need an explanation except, perhaps, Lycophron (ca. 300–250* B.C.), *an Alexandrian grammarian and poet; Lucan* (A.D. 39–65), *author of the unfinished poem on the civil war between Caesar and Pompey,* Pharsalia; *Tibullus (54?–19* B.C.), *a Roman poet especially famous for his elegies; Ausonius (d. ca.* A.D. 395), *first tutor of Gratian, then governor of Gaul, later poet, best known for the river poem,* Mosella; *Statius (ca.* A.D. 45–96), *court poet of Domitian, and much admired during the Middle Ages for his epic poem,* Thebais.

82 VATABLUS . . . SYMANCHA *All were professors whose names pedants would be likely to use. Vatablus or François Vatable (d. 1547?) of the Royal College of France was an authority on Hebrew, the Bible, and Aristotle. Pompanatius or*

Pietro Pomponazzi (1462–1524?) was a philosopher of Padua whose tract on immortality was condemned as heretical. Symancha or Didacus de Simancas (ca. 1565) was a jurist and bishop of Salamanca.

99 POETS *Back of this exchange, and not entirely obscured by Daw's idiocy, lies a genuine conflict between professional writers and gentlemen. The sixteenth-century writer who lived by his pen lacked the prestige of gentleman authors who wrote for each other in the Inns of Court and the univeristies or, as with Sidney's* Arcadia, *for the enjoyment of friends and relatives. Except for scholarly work, gentlemen customarily did not think it proper to print what they had written. None of Sidney's literary works, for instance, was printed during his lifetime. Daw's comment reflects this aristocratic disdain for publishing, but he charac-teristically confuses the point by inverting the distinction between versifiers and poets: to him poets are poor fellows who live by their verse, whereas versifiers are great wits who do not need to write to live. The "stigma of print" began to lose its force in the seventeenth century, partly through the example of Jonson, who had the literary and personal prestige to win for himself a position as poet, man of letters, and gentleman. See J. W. Saunders, "The Stigma of Print: a Note on the Social Basis of Tudor Poetry,"* Essays in Criticism, *1 (April, 1951): 139–64.*

106 SIDNEY *Sidney's sister, the Countess of Pembroke, thought enough of his work and of "poetry" to permit publication of his major works after his death in 1586, among them his sonnets (1591) and his prose epic, published as the* Countess of Pembrokes Arcadia *(1590, 1593, 1598).*

Act II, Scene 4

96 QUARTER-FEAST *The responses of Clerimont and Truewit suggest that Daw has attempted a sarcastic witticism at his friend La Foole's expense. It seems to have something to do with the nature of quarter-days, the days on which pay-ments of rent and other quarterly charges fall due. Daw may be saying that La Foole's "friends" whom he is trying to muster to his feast are really people who come only because, owing him money or renting from him, they do not wish to offend him.*

Act II, Scene 5

85–113 *In this soliloquy Jonson distills an experience often treated at greater length by Elizabethan and Jacobean pamphleteers and dramatists—what it means to be* down and out in London, or how to live on nothing at all. In Morose's idealization of Dauphine's fate, everything that could happen to a knight who is down and out would happen to him: his credit lost, his goods seized, his very future in the hands of money-lenders; too poor to flee, too ragged to seduce even a citizen's wife, and not clever enough at cheating to keep from being forced to live off a whore. Having sunk so low, he becomes a "shark" (a cheat and a sponger), who, as John Earle describes him, "Amongst other of his shipwracks . . . has happily lost shame, and this want supplies him. No man puts his brain to more use than he, for his life is a daily invention, and each meal a new stratagem." [13]

104 COMMODITY Among the many low actions which Morose foresees for the disinherited Dauphine, one of the worst is the fate which sometimes awaited Jacobean spendthrifts. To evade the statute of 1572 which limited interest to ten per cent, moneylenders worked out the "commodity swindle" by which the borrower was compelled to take part of the sum he wanted in inferior or even damaged goods and to sign a bond, often with other borrowers, to pay the amount at some future date. Then he was forced to sell this "commodity," usually either to the usurer or to some confederate of the usurer, and of course at a much lower price than he had paid. If he had signed as "the tenth name in the bond," he would have been the tenth man to receive money from the sale of such a commodity—hence, little if any money. See Thomas Dekker, Lanthorn and Candlelight (1608), chapter 4; and The Works of Thomas Nashe, ed. R. B. McKerrow and F. P. Wilson (Oxford, 1958), 2: 93–95; 4: 230.

108 HOW This word is italicized in the Folio, suggesting a sly personal reference, perhaps to Edmund Howes, the chronicler who continued John Stow's Annales and who seems to have had at least a literary fame as a reveler.

Act II, Scene 6

30 BRIDAL The Folio has "bride-ale," which the OED calls "a conscious retention or restoration of the earlier analytical form of bridal"; as such, it referred to "a wedding feast of the Old English type," which emphasized ale-drinking. At one time a bride from a poor family sold ale to the guests, who paid whatever they chose.[14]

---

13. Microcosmography (London, 1934), p. 24.
14. Shakespeare's England, ed. Sir Walter Raleigh (London, 1916), 2:148.

55 BEAR GARDEN *This pit for bear-baiting and the Paris Garden which Mrs. Otter refers to in III.1.14 and 25 were not actually the same place, though they were often associated and even identified. Joris Hoefnagel's map of London (drawn about 1570), which appeared in* Civitates Orbis Terrarum *(an atlas published by Braun and Hogenberg at Cologne from 1572 to 1618), makes clear that the Bear Garden was just east of Paris (or Parish) Garden on the Bank-side in Southwark. Probably the two were closely associated in the language of gentlemen who took the ferry from Blackfriars landing straight across the Thames to the landing at Paris Garden in order to see the baiting at the adjacent Bear Garden. Hoefnagel marks separately two rings, one called " The Boull-baytying," the other " The Beare-baytying." Stow may be referring to these rings when he describes the "two Beare gardens, the olde and new places wherein be kept Beares, Buls and other beastes to be bayted . . . in plottes of ground, scaffolded about for the Beholders to stand safe."* 15

Act III, Scene 1

4 YOU . . . BEST *An idiom in which the "you" was originally dative. Depending on how the tone is understood, a rough paraphrase might be either, " You think you can bait me . . . !" or, "You should try baiting me (instead of the courtiers) . . . ;" in any case, Otter falls "under correction."*

7 WHITSUNTIDE *The week following Whitsunday was a time of festivity. Especially merry was the Whitsun Ale, which Mrs. Otter may be alluding to here. As on all holidays, velvet caps would be worn. The staff may be explained by a custom in Oxfordshire on Whit Monday: a clown called the Squire led a procession around town, carrying a staff with a calf's tail at one end and a bladder at the other, which he used to belabor the bystanders.* 16 *The staff, too, would be another of Mrs. Otter's ways of emphasizing her husband's servile status since peasants and constables carried staffs, while gentlemen wore swords.*

13 RERUM NATURA *Otter appears to use the Latin phrase correctly, if awkwardly, his meaning being " in the physical universe;" it would make better sense in this context if he meant " as a fact of nature, a natural phenomenon," but there is no need to suspect him of sense, especially in Latin.*

15. John Stow, *The Survey of London*, ed. C. L. Kingsford (London, 1908), 2:54. See also E. K. Chambers, *The Elizabethan Stage* (Oxford, 1923), 2:449–71.

16. P. Ditchfield, *Old English Customs* (London, 1901), p. 124.

Notes, Act III Scene 2

21 POETARIUM PEGASUS *The gloss in H & S compares the phrase "the Poets' Horse" (misprinted as "Poet's"), from Jonson's Verses over the door of the Apollo, where the inspiring power is identified more closely with Otter's cups than with mythology:*

> *Wine it is the milk of Venus*
> *And the Poets' Horse accounted.*
> *Ply it and you all are mounted.*

35 THREE . . . WORSTED *Servants in Jacobean England usually owned about three suits of clothes. Edgar in King Lear describes himself as having been a "serving-man" with "three suits to his back" (III.4.133). Silk stockings, then fashionable and expensive, would have been worn by servants only on special holidays; otherwise, worsted.*

Act III, Scene 2

6 SIC . . . SUPERIS *Otter, of course, is acknowledging the superior power to which he and his cups are most immediately subject—his wife—and to do so in Latin allows him to be humble and pompous at the same time. The phrase itself, as noted in H & S, is the opposite of the Vergilian "Dis aliter visum est" ("the gods decreed otherwise," Aeneid II.428) which Seneca advises the Stoic to repeat to himself as armament against the blows of inconstant fortune (Epistles XCVIII.5). Perhaps there is an echo of Horace's "Sic visum Veneri" ("such is the decree of Venus,") for, he says, the goddess enjoys yoking ill-matched bodies and souls together as a cruel joke (Odes I.xxxiii.10–12).*

39 BULRUSH . . . PICKED *L. A. Beaurline ingeniously if not altogether convincingly cites Sir Thomas Browne's description of the "bumping" sound made by the bittern's "putting its bill into a reed" (Vulgar Errors, III.27.4).*

51 DREAM . . . PAGEANT *Mrs. Otter's dream—dreams were still thought to be prophetic—reveals her social aspirations. Apparently she dreams of the pageant given on the Lord Mayor's day when, in great magnificence for a man not born to ceremony or display, a citizen is elevated to that peculiarly British station, a Mayor who is a Lord. Significantly, Mrs. Otter refers to "My Lady Mayoress."*

57 IT *Mrs. Otter's confused pronoun references reveal the confusion of her mind, as Clerimont's comment (l. 56) suggests. Is it her dream that has done her "many affronts," or Lady Haughty's explanation of it, or her own reaction to either the*

186

*dream or the explanation? Most probably it is the city itself, as Clerimont con-
cludes in l. 68. Mrs. Otter seems, or pretends, to think that her dreaming leads to
the city's affronts to her dignity and clothes, while providing her a rhetorical
occasion for displaying them.*

64 DOUBLET *Normally, man's attire. Phillip Stubbes calls women who wear men's
apparel such as doublets and jerkins* "Hermaphroditi, *that is, Monsters of bothe
kindes, half women, half men.*" [17]

Act III, Scene 3

20 JOVIAL *This term is regularly italicized in the Folio text (see ll. 27 and 35, below,
and IV.2.32–62), presumably to stress Daw's affectation of a fairly recent loan
word, and his ignorance of the word's astrological implications. As the helplessly
susceptible victim of* "influences." *Daw seems to caricature the determinism
implicit in astrology, and to anticipate the related Stoic doctrine of fate imposed
upon him later (IV.5.244 ff.). The influences to which he is subject, of course,
are not from the stars, but from Truewit and Clerimont. Their method of making
him* "jovial" *now, as it includes their plans for the wedding party, suggests an
astrological cure for the melancholy they had caused earlier (II.4.123 ff.): food,
wine, music, and mirth were among the means prescribed for attracting the
influences of benign planets—jovial, solar, venereal, mercurial—needed to counter
the dangerous Saturnine influences threatening the morose or melancholy man.
See D. P. Walker,* Spiritual and Demonic Magic from Ficino to Cam-
panella *(London, 1958), chap. 1.*

29 SAVER . . . MAIN *"The main" was a term used in Hazard, a game very popular
in the seventeenth century and still popular in the debased form known as craps.
It was played with two dice and by any number of players, one of whom, the
caster, threw the dice. He first threw to determine the "main" point, which had
to be a 4, 5, 6, 7, 8, or 9. Once the main was established, he threw to determine
the "chance point"—any number from 4 to 10. In these throws to establish the
"chance point" he could lose the stakes outright if he threw a 2 or 3 (known as
Crabs—hence, craps) or, in certain circumstances, an 11 or 12. In these throws,
too, he could win the stakes if he threw his "main point," or if he threw a 12
when the main point was a 6 or an 8, or an 11 when the main point was a 7.*

---

17. *Phillip Stubbes's Anatomie of Abuses in England,* ed. F. Furnivall (London,
1877–79), p. 73.

These winning throws are called "nicks." Once the chance point was determined, the caster continued to throw until either the chance point came up, and he won the stakes on the table, or the main point came up, and he lost them. A "saver," also a gaming term, was defined by Johnson as "one who escapes loss, though without gain." In short, Clerimont is telling Daw to compensate for the loss of his dignity as well as his mistress by winning his main point—that is, setting back La Foole by going to a dinner which Epicoene would give in his honor.

52 INHUMANLY *The Folio spelling was "inhumanely." "Human" was often spelled "humane" before the eighteenth century when the two words became distinctly different in pronunciation and meaning. Before they were separated, a human being was apparently expected to be humane. Or, more exactly, his behavior toward others was expected to be such as befits a man—that is, civil, courteous, gentle, kindly.*

115 EX . . . METAMORPHOSI *Callisto appears in the* Metamorphoses, *II.401–507, but Ovid's treatment of the Pasiphae story is in the* Ars Amatoria, *I.295–326. Otter "latins it" like Cutbeard, but perhaps the point lies less in his error than in the emphasis given, by the use of Ovid's title, to the various metamorphoses in the play: a girl turns out to be a boy; a husband tries to pass himself off as no man; knights, who are expected to be courageous, prove to be cowards; women, theoretically modest, pursue men; a nephew is transformed from a nearly penniless ward to the guardian of his uncle; a barber and an ex-bearkeeper are "exalted" into a canon lawyer and a divine. Such transformations are comic because they violate the surface decorum of Renaissance society. Generally, Renaissance philosophy held that a man's true place in the scheme of things depended on his own nature and on the function that that nature ordained for him; to alter one's nature or function—indeed, even to try—was to lose one's place and to lose one's way.*

Act III, Scene 5

21–22 CONDUIT . . . INFANTRY *"Conduit" then referred both to the pipe or channel through which water circulated and to its source, where water-carriers as well as ordinary citizens would gather to draw the city water and exchange the city news. A "bakehouse," in which bread was made and sold, was another place for the daily exchange of gossip and news. By "the infantry that follow the court" Truewit apparently means the household drudges who ride with the kitchen utensils on royal progresses. In two masques,* Mercury Vindicated, *l. 86* and Love Restored, *l. 118, Jonson refers to them as the "Black Guard" because of their association with fires, spits, and pans.*

63–107 *The burlesque invective, which Truewit has suggested to Morose (ll. 58 ff.), is a convention of comical satire. Jonson, however, has heightened the comic effect by alternating lines of dialogue between the two speakers to suggest the classical convention called* stichomythia, *associated in this period primarily with Senecan tragedy. Its conventional function, as an expression of tension or conflict between the speakers, is comically masked or suspended until Morose is exhausted, and his protests alternate with Truewit's insistent proliferation of still more "curses."*

Act III, Scene 6

64–80 ENSIGNS . . . MASQUE *Lady Haughty complains that, in his haste to marry Epicoene, Morose has neglected all the customs of a proper marriage: there are no gloves (usually given to all guests) or scarves (sometimes given to the ladies); the bride and groom have not chosen their colors, which their respective guests might wear to honor them; no formal wedding song has been written, no wedding masque performed; the young men have had no opportunity to try to possess the bride's garters. Most unfortunate of all, the bride and groom have forfeited the gifts of silver and gold plate, and perhaps some friends, through Morose's breach of decorum.*

Act IV, Scene 1

23 SADDLER'S HORSE *Morose astraddle the cross-beam is grotesquely compared with the Elizabethan sign for a saddler's shop, which consisted of a booted leg hanging down each side of a "horse" jutting out into the street.*

32–113 *Truewit's advice on how women should dress to attract men and how men should act to win women draws heavily on Ovid's Ars* Amatoria. *H & S quote the relevant passages in their commentary (8: 28–32). Jonson's use of Ovid reveals even more fully than his use of Juvenal (in II.2.14–125) how resourceful he could be in handling other literary works. In general, he makes three kinds of changes. First, he may keep the general point that Ovid makes, but change the particulars. Thus, Ovid refers to statues in the Roman theater when he describes how women ought to dress and make themselves up in private (Ars, III.225–34); Jonson changes the reference to the new statues at Aldgate (see I.1.110–111 N.). Second, he may add significant details that alter—sometimes radically—the original tone of the passage. Ovid emphasizes the attractive appearance that careful*

189

grooming can create, but when Truewit adds the wigs, the false teeth, and the eyebrows (I.1.106–07), he reduces the lady's preparation to absurdity by turning it, as Jonas Barish points out, into a "catalogue of grotesque appliances." Finally, Jonson may altogether suppress whatever in his source would not help to create the effect he wanted. For this reason, apparently, he cut away all the allusions to myth (except to Penelope) and most references to external nature which elevate the tone of Ovid's advice. Here again Professor Barish's article, cited in the note for II.2.14–125, is especially helpful, though we are not forced to conclude as he does that Truewit's manifestations as fashionable gallant, dupe of fashion, and Stoic moralizer are impossible to reconcile. Truewit is never thoroughly any of these. He is, instead, always a cool observer of a life he plays with, while rejecting its values. Jonson's handling of Truewit is far from irresolute; rather, it constitutes a triumph of artistic control. Like Jonson, Truewit can use both Juvenal and Ovid without limiting himself to the vision of either.

51 AMADIS . . . QUIXOTE *Amadis is a wonderfully preposterous Spanish chivalric romance, translated first into French and later into English (Book I by one of Jonson's favorite dunces, Anthony Munday, in 1590). Only the first part of* Don Quixote *had appeared by 1609. Jonson couples these two romances in several places, but we need not conclude that he had the same contempt for* Quixote *that he obviously had for* Amadis.

81 ALL WAYS *Both the first Folio and the Quarto have one word here—"alwaies"— which Simpson regards as a misprint (H & S, 5:148) and which Whalley (following Upton?) revised to "all ways" in 1756 (Works of Ben Jonson, ed. Peter Whalley [London, 1756]). Whalley's reading seems preferable to the Folio's not merely because it echoes Ovid's lines in Ars Amatoria, I.755–56, "Sed sunt diversa puellis / Pectora: mille animos excipe mille modis" (which Rolfe Humphries translates, "the hearts of the girls! How they differ! / Use a thousand means, since there are thousands of ends."), but also because it makes more sense to say that "all women are not to be taken all ways" than ". . . always taken."*

Act IV, Scene 2

4–5 BULL . . . BAIT *Aurelia Henry sees this scene as a parody of bear-baiting.*[18] *Certainly there are a number of allusions to the baiting of bears and bulls here.*

---

18. *Epicoene.* Yale Studies in English, 31 (New Haven, 1906), p. 228.

Earlier, Truewit uses the baiting metaphors to describe Mrs. Otter's plaguing of Otter (III.1.43, 47). So often does one character plague another that we can view baiting as a recurrent motif in the whole play. See the Introduction, p. 3.

66 NUNC . . . LIBERO *An especially ironic allusion because Horace's ode celebrates the fall of Cleopatra, that frenzied queen, and Otter makes it just as his own fatal Cleopatra is about to descend on him.*

71 CLOGDOGDO *A perplexing word. H & S suggest it is Bear Garden slang. Upton thought it meant a clog—that is, a heavy piece of wood attached to the leg or neck to impede motion—which is proper only for a dog. Howard Staunton thought it equivalent to the "trash" in Prospero's phrase, "to trash for over-topping" (Variorum Tempest, I.2.98; Works of W. Shakespeare, ed. H. Staunton [London, 1879], 4:454): that is, a weight tied around the hound's neck to train it.*

73 MALA BESTIA *This phrase appears both in Plautus, Bacchides, I.1.21, and in Catullus, LXIX.7–8. If it echoes either passage, the Catullus is more probable because in it a certain Rufus is told he is so horrid that no dainty woman wants to come to his arms.*

89–90 TEETH . . . HER *The place-names seem to be chosen, in part, for what they suggest about Mrs. Otter's pieced beauty: e.g., her false teeth are probably black, her false eyebrows coarse, as if plaited like strands of rope, her false hair turned white (and possibly tarnished?). Otter has found "art's hidden causes" all over town, and all over Mrs. Otter as well—"All is not sweet, all is not sound." She seems to embody the "adulteries of art" as disdained by Clerimont and defended by Truewit (see I.1.77 ff. and IV.1.33 ff.), but in her case it is difficult to determine whether art adulterates nature, or nature adulterates art.*

96–98 QUARTERS . . . QUARTERS *Otter thinks of his wife, after her alarm to the whole house, as withdrawn to her personal quarters but still making herself heard, like a clock striking the quarter hours. In picking up his phrases, Mrs. Otter may mean to use them as no more than blunt instruments (cf. her use of "nature" in III.1.14–15) but the context suggests that her "quarters" are the strokes or blows in fencing that were called "quarter-blows."*

97–98 SD SHE . . . HIM *Jacobeans would have thought Mrs. Otter's treatment of Capt. Otter an inversion of the normal. Their domestic books invariably recommended conduct for both husband and wife the reverse of the Otters'. A famous book by the Puritan preacher, William Gouge, set down domestic duties that few*

Notes, Act IV Scene 3

Englishmen would have disagreed with: a wife was subject to her husband and was
expected to be modest, meek, and obedient; a husband was expected to teach his
wife her place if she did not know it and to maintain his authority up to the
point of beating her.[19] *This marital norm would have made the marriage of the*
Otters the comic irony that Truewit and Clerimont find it to be.

117 ILL MAY DAY *Any May first, with its Maypole dancing and merrymaking,*
would be an ill day to a man who hated noise, but Morose may be alluding to
May 1, 1517, when the apprentices of London rose against the privileged
foreigners whose advantages in trade angered them. Since the apprentices were
imprisoned for rioting, that May day came to be called "Evil" or "Ill." See
Stow, The Survey of London, *ed. C. L. Kingsford, 1:143, 152.*

    Act IV, Scene 3

28 SD *Gifford's direction for the entrance of Clerimont and Truewit here is misplaced*
by H & S to l. 24 of the following scene, clearly a slip since Truewit has an
aside in this scene, l. 35.

33-34 THAMES . . . TORCHES *Daw and La Foole draw on both literary and popular*
tradition for their gnomic wisdom. Most of the dialogue from l. 31 to the end of
the scene is modeled on Book III of Ovid's Ars Amatoria, *the speeches of Daw*
and La Foole corresponding to ll. 93-94.

> Quis vetet adposito lumen de lumine sumi?
> Quisve cavo vastas in mare servet aquas?

> *(Who would prohibit light to be taken from the offered lamp?*
> *Or who would keep account of the vast waters of the deep sea?)*

The popular sources are proverbial aphorisms like the quotation from Cawdrey
in the gloss for l. 34, or the example in M. P. Tilley, A Dictionary of the
Proverbs in England in the Sixteenth and Seventeenth Centuries (*Ann*
Arbor, 1950), *cited by Beaurline.*

    An awareness of sources and analogues is essential here, for it reinforces the
rhetorical effect toward which the whole scene tends, suggesting a kind of speech
in which words are used as if virtually severed from sense ("the life and soule of
Language, without which all words are dead" as Jonson said in Discoveries),

---

19. Gouge, *Of Domesticall Duties: Eight Treatises* (London, 1634).

and meaning seems to lie in the fact of something having been said before, not in saying it now. See Introduction, pp. 12–14.

49 HOBBY-HORSE *Characteristic of Jonson's language is the way this figurative expression is thrown back vividly to its original meaning. Originally, a "hobby" was a small or middle-sized horse of Irish breed. Gradually, up to the seventeenth century, "hobby-horse" acquired a series of meanings: the figure of a horse fastened about the waist of a performer in a morris-dance; a stick with a horse's head which children could ride; a person who plays ridiculous antics or a foolish fellow; a lustful person or a loose woman. Jonson refers to the next to the last of these, and by modifying it with "neighing" reminds one of its literal base without losing its figurative extension—indeed, "neighing" helps to realize that figure concretely.*

Act IV, Scene 4

12–14 BELFRY ... BILLINGSGATE *Morose catalogs the noisiest places in Jacobean England. Some of them, such as a belfry or a cockpit, London Bridge or Paris Garden (see II.6.55 and N.) would have been, for obvious reasons, purgatories to Morose. In Westminster Hall were not only courts of justice—Exchequer and Chancery as well as common law—but also shops rented to booksellers, stationers, and seamstresses; in short, the endless clamor of litigation and commerce. His mention of Tower Wharf is comic not so much because it would be actually any noisier than an ordinary wharf as because it would be potentially so: ordnance was stored there (see I.2.14–15). Billingsgate was an especially busy wharf, whose fish markets and fishwives became notorious for rough and loud language soon after its establishment in 1599. Morose reveals his courtly pretensions by citing one country sport—hunting the stag—which with baying hounds, hunter's horns, and echoing woods could have been an exquisite and (considering King James's interest in hunting) frequent torture to one of Morose's humor.*

46 INTESTATE *Strictly and legally, Morose is wrong. If a husband died intestate, leaving a wife but no child, his widow was entitled to only half his estate, the remainder going to the next of kin. See Paul Clarkson and Clyde Warren,* The Law of Property in Shakespeare and the Elizabethan Drama *(Baltimore, 1947), p. 194, n. 8.*

50 MELANCHOLY *H & S claims that here the word should be understood in its ancient sense of passion or frenzy. Certainly the sparkling eyes suggest the lunatic, and Epicoene explicitly refers to running mad (l. 40). But several phrases*

connote the Elizabethan melancholy induced by frustrated or lost love. One is Morose's direct denial of love as a cause of his anger. Another is his discolored skin (ll. 48–49), which, as Jacques Ferrand explains in his Erotomania *(translated from the French in 1640, but written about 1612), was a prominent mark of love melancholy. Viola's "green and yellow melancholy" in* Twelfth Night *gives the conventional picture of love-sickness. Actually, as Lawrence Babb points out in* The Elizabethan Malady *(East Lansing, Mich., 1951), some derangement of mind was thought necessarily to accompany such sickness. See also R. Klibansky, E. Panofsky, F. Saxl,* Saturn and Melancholy *(New York, 1964), esp. pp. 127–30.*

52 PLINY . . . PARACELSUS *These are odd choices to invoke as standard medical authorities: Jonson cites them among his sources for the witches in* The Masque of Queens. *In addition, the thirty-seven books of Pliny and the idiosyncratic obscurity of Paracelsus (which Latin translation could neither render nor remove) are as unlikely reading for Daw as the sackful of names in II.3, and more pointedly incongruous. The noisy controversy touched off by these writings amounted to a virtual battle of the books, of ancients against moderns. Since the latter part of the sixteenth century, this argument—between the disciples of Paracelsus and the adherents of the traditional orthodoxy of Aristotle, Avicenna, and Galen—had been growing in intensity. Though primarily medical, the argument focused on philosophical, political, and religious issues as well. (See Allen G. Debus,* The English Paracelsians, *London, 1965.) The name "Paracelsus" became practically synonymous with "war"; its owner was notoriously bad-tempered and contentious. His career seemed a long series of ruinous quarrels—with princes and patrons, patients and professional colleagues. At odds with society, a solitary eccentric, widely believed to be both impotent and misogynistic, Paracelsus is strangely suggestive of Morose; but as a model for his condition, not a cure.*

59–64 DISEASE . . . DELIRIUM *In ll. 59–61 Daw manages to say the same thing in six different terms drawn from three different languages—Morose is mad; he is so mad that he's beside himself, having gone out* (egressio) *of himself. Then in ll. 63–64 Daw wonders if Morose may not be only temporarily delirious—that is, suffering from phrenetis, an inflammation of the brain.*

85 DONI'S PHILOSOPHY *Sir Amorous characteristically confuses the old beast fable of Reynard the Fox with the collection of Oriental stories now known as the "fables of Bidpai." These latter apologues, after a series of translations out of Persian, Arabic, Greek, and Latin, reached modern languages in the Italian rendering (1552) by Antonio Francesco Doni (1513–74) and in Sir Thomas North's English translation of Doni called* The Moral Philosophie of Doni

(1570). *Foxes appear as characters in several of Bidpai's stories, but none has the suavity of Reynard.*

165 SET . . . PRIMERO *The* OED *says that the precise meaning of this phrase is not clear (see "Nick," IV.11). We might observe, first, that, as usual, La Foole has confused things—here, a card game and a dice game. Primero was a very fashionable card game from about 1530 to 1640 and later so rarely played as to be nearly unknown. "Nick" is a special term in hazard, a dice game already explained (see III.3.29 N.). La Foole seems to mean that the penniless Dauphine had kept on "nicking" him, with the implication that it has been done dishonestly.*

Act IV, Scene 5

42 CENTAURS *At the wedding feast of Pirithous, half-brother of the Centaurs and King of the Lapithae, and Hippodamia, the Centaurs tried to carry off the bride, and were prevented only after a bloody battle.*

88–89 SET . . . POSSESSION *Transfer of property was not legally completed unless and until the purchaser actually took physical possession, or in attempting to do so was prevented by force—a frequent occurrence in this period.*

99 MAN . . . YEAR *According to the Statute for Arms and Armour passed in 1557, every nobleman and gentleman was required to keep, according to his means, a fixed number of weapons, horses, and suits of armor. Since the highest income named by the Act was one thousand pounds, Truewit may be trying to frighten the already chattering Daw by suggesting, illogically, that La Foole is carrying even more than twice as many weapons as the maximum required by law.*

232–33 MAGIS . . . FERIENDO. *H & S cites Joseph Wybarne's comment in* The New Age of Old Names *(1609) on the way the spirit of revenge has borrowed the vizard of Fortitude. Wybarne claims that the heathens will condemn Christians before the true Minos for their "revengefull desires, masked with the Name of Fortitude, which is notwithstanding taken* a Ferendo *not* a feriendo, nam patiendo, male non faciendo, fortes sumus" *(p. 28). This Latin phrase may appear, as the idea it expresses certainly does, in Renaissance discussions of Stoicism.*

308–09 DAMON AND PYTHIAS *Then as now, this pair connoted a type of perfect friendship. Damon gave himself as a hostage for his friend Pythias, who had been condemned for plotting against Dionysius of Syracuse. Dionysius was so moved by this unselfishness, as well as the fidelity of Pythias, who returned to liberate Damon, that he released them both.*

Act IV, Scene 6

1 SD HAVING DISCOVERED *Jonson's stage direction leaves it up to the director precisely when he would have Haughty, Centaure, Mavis, Mrs. Otter, Epicoene, Trusty, and Clerimont enter on the upper stage to watch Truewit's demonstration of the cowardice of Daw and La Foole. Gifford's choice (at l. 288 in scene 5) is not followed here because, entering then, the ladies would see only the cowardice of Sir Amorous and not that of Sir John. A better place might be l. 243 in scene 5, just in time to hear Truewit's counsel to Daw.*

68 PYLADES AND ORESTES *Orestes became an intimate friend of Pylades when he fled to the court of Pylades' father, Strophius, the king of Phocis, after his own father, Agamemnon, had been murdered by his mother, Clytemnestra, and her lover, Aegisthus. Pylades helped his friend execute the murderers. A further instance of their friendship occurred in the land of the Tauri (apparently, the modern Crimea) where they were captured and were about to be sacrificed. Learning that one could be saved, Orestes insisted on being sacrificed, but both were saved when the resident priestess, who proved to be Orestes' own sister, Iphigenia, discovered their identities, freed both, and fled with them.*

Act IV, Scene 7

5 BEGGED *In the early Jacobean age laws regarding manslaughter with swords and daggers were especially severe because of the frequent quarrels between Englishmen and Scottish favorites of James I who came south after his accession in 1603. The property of a criminal or even one suspected of a crime could be confiscated by the crown and then "begged"—that is, petitioned for—in the courts. See Black-stone,* Commentaries, 4, *chap. 14.*

Act V, Scene 1

11 SCRIVENER *Clerimont pretends anger at Mavis's insinuation that he might carry pen and ink, the tools in trade of scriveners, an occupation beneath the dignity of a gentleman; but also, in legal matters, often tainted by dishonesty.*

Act V, Scene 2

1 PRICE ... ESTIMATION *Haughty's effusive speech illustrates her lack of discrimination. "Price" and "estimation," though not exactly synonymous, are too similar to warrant this usage; and soon after (ll. 5, 10, 15–16) Haughty pairs "love" and "affect," "rank" and "society," "flat" and "dully" with the same extravagance. She is also deaf to Dauphine's ironic play on "price" in l. 6.*

Act V, Scene 3

10 DOCTOR ... PARSON *Both doctors of canon law and parsons deserved the title of " Master," a term of respect for their rank, but the superfluous use of these titles here emphasizes the ludicrousness of their pretense. The distinction between Otter, the "divine," and Cutbeard, the "canon lawyer," is that Otter pretends to judge on the basis of practical experience ("positive Divinity," l. 37) and Cutbeard on the basis of canon law. Part of the fun lies in the tone each adopts: Cutbeard sounds like a medieval Catholic and Otter a Puritan Protestant.*

62 DIVORTIUM *By pairing Otter and Cutbeard in this scene and making each comment antiphonally on the other's remarks, Jonson manages to use the ecclesiastical terminology comically and still make it understandable to an audience for the most part unschooled in Latin and Greek. Thus when Cutbeard describes the first of the twelve impediments to a valid marriage, Otter pedantically clarifies its meaning for the agonized Morose—and for us (ll. 79–90).*

66 CANON LAW *Strictly speaking, canon law and the common law which derives from it do not "afford" divorce at all; they only recognize certain obstacles to a valid marriage. Such impediments cause a "nullity"—that is, an annulment, which in effect decrees that no marriage has taken place. The "verse" to which Otter refers appears in the* "Supplementum ad Tertiam Partem" *of Aquinas's* Summa Theologica *at least as early as the Venice edition of 1486. In her edition of* Epicoene *Aurelia Henry quotes the verse given in the 1619 Rome edition of the* Summa.

> Error, conditio, votum, cognatio, crimen,
> Cultus disparitas, vis, ordo, ligamen, honestas,
> Si sis affinis, si forte coire nequibis,
> Haec socianda vetant connubia, facta retractant.

These lines are explained, item by item, in the dialogue. Upton had previously referred to this passage but did not note that it appears in editions of the Summa. *Probably the verse was familiar enough so that many Jacobeans could recognize Otter's use of the last line in ll. 184–85 and Cutbeard's allusion to the next to the last line in l. 155. Englishmen then would have been especially aware of these impediments because the legitimacy of Queen Elizabeth had depended precisely on them, affinity being the impediment to Henry VIII's marriage with Catherine of Aragon and therefore the means by which his union with Elizabeth's mother, Anne Boleyn, could be legalized. St. Thomas's discussion of these impediments appears in the* Summa Theologica, trans. by the Fathers of the English Dominican *Province (London, 1932), Third Part (Supplement), QQ 51–67. Since most of the Latin in this scene is either translated in the dialogue or too simple to perplex even the un-Latinate, only the especially obscure lines will be glossed.*[20]

106 DISCIPLINE *Generally, the system by which the practice of a church is regulated; more specifically, in the seventeenth century, the ecclesiastical polity of the Puritan or Presbyterian sects.*

143–52 AFFINITAS . . . GENERATUR *The sense here is that an impediment may arise from fornication too because fornication can involve as true an "affinity" as that which arises from legitimate marriage (l. 146). True affinity arises from the fact that two persons are made one flesh by intercourse (ll. 147–48). Within certain prohibited degrees of relationship, no relative of one person guilty of fornication could marry the other guilty person. Otter gives one rationalization of this impediment when he says that one who generates through fornication is truly a father, and the son who is generated is truly a son (ll. 148–53).*

Act V Scene 4

20 MANKIND *As a form of the adjective "mankeen," used primarily of animals likely to attack men, the word means "fierce, cruel, savage." The gloss in H & S is restricted to this meaning, and specifically excludes "masculine" as a possibility. But as used by Morose to describe the Ladies Collegiate, in this epicoene context, "mankind" seems to imply lack of femininity. See Introduction, pp. 15–17.*

---

20. Thomas Kranidas thinks it "highly probable" that Jonson revised the fifth act in 1613 or later to add or point up two allusions (V.3.170–76 and V.4.48–61) to the celebrated divorce trial of the Earl and Countess of Essex in that year. See "Possible Revisions or Additions in Jonson's *Epicoene,*" *Anglia,* 83 (1965):451–53.

Appendix: Sources, Stage History, and Text

SOURCES

The main plot devices of *Epicoene* seem to derive from two sources. For the character and situation of Morose, Jonson appears to have used a rhetorical exercise or demonstration by Libanius, a fourth-century Greek whose school of rhetoric at Constantinople had the favor of the Emperor Julian (the Apostate). In the *Sixth Declamation* of Libanius, a desperate husband pleads for legal permission to commit suicide in order to be rid of a wife he was deluded into marrying in the belief that she spoke softly and seldom, only to discover that she is insatiably garrulous. In 1606 an edition of Libanius' works was published in Paris, with the Greek and a Latin translation in parallel columns; the husband's name is translated as Morosus.

The trick of disguising a boy as a bride is considered by Aurelia Henry and by Herford and Simpson to be based on Plautus' *Casina*. A better case has been made for Aretino's *Il Marescalco*, in which an amusement-seeking nobleman arranges a "marriage" (with a disguised page) for a misogynistic gentleman-usher, whose increasingly frantic efforts to escape such a fate culminate in a public declaration of impotence (see the essay below by O. J. Campbell in the list of selected reading).

To enhance the comic value of his plot, Jonson as usual exploited a variety of materials. The striking use of Ovid and Juvenal, indicated in the notes to this edition, has been discussed in detail by Jonas Barish (see the list below of selected reading.).

STAGE HISTORY

Epicoene was first acted by the Children of her Majesty's Revels at White-friars, either in 1609 (as the title page in the Folio of 1616 says) or early in

Appendix

1610, as E. K. Chambers speculates. Since this company of boy actors, formerly the Children of the Chapel, was not entitled to call itself the Children of the Queen's Revels before its patent of January 4, 1610, early in 1610 may be the better date. The play seems to have run into some trouble on its first or on an early performance—trouble I shall describe below. No other performances are recorded (though some may have taken place) before 1636, when it was presented twice at the Court of St. James, first on February 18, 1635/36, then on April 21. Perhaps only with the Restoration of the Stuarts did it come into its own. It was the first play recorded as having been publicly performed after the return of the king on May 25, 1660 (probably early in June, 1660, at the Red Bull in Clerkenwell) as well as the first presented at court in the Cockpit at Whitehall on November 19, 1660, and it also became a model for the Restoration comedy of manners, in part because Dryden praised it so highly in his *Essay of Dramatic Poesy.* R. G. Noyes records about a hundred performances from 1660 to 1752. Since then, except for infrequent revivals, usually in the form of adaptations, it has left the stage to its collateral descendents.[1] Curiously, it prospered, relatively, in other countries during the very years of its neglect in England. It was translated or "adapted" into Portugese in 1769, into German by Ludwig Tieck in 1800, into Russian by R. Blokh in 1921, and into French by Marcel Achard in 1926. Several composers have found the comic idea of its plot, if not the plot itself, attractive—among them, Salieri in 1800 for his *Angliolina ossia il matrimonio fer susurro* and Richard Strauss in 1935 for his *Die schweigsame Frau.*

The trouble already mentioned arose apparently because of an alleged slighting reference to Lady Arabella Stuart (denied by Jonson) in La Foole's remark about "the Prince of Moldavia" and "his mistress, Mistress Epicoene" (V.1.20–21). The passage seems harmless enough if "his mistress" is taken to refer to Epicoene's relationship to Daw before her marriage to Morose. But if, as the syntax allows, "his" refers to the Prince of Moldavia, and if "Mistress Epicoene" is taken, as apparently it was, to allude to someone connected with the Prince, then another and more pointed interpretation is possible. Briefly, the story is this. The self-styled "Prince" was an impostor,

---

1. See Robert Noyes, *Ben Jonson on the English Stage, 1660–1776,* Harvard Studies in English, 17 (Cambridge, 1935), pp. 173–221, and *H & S,* 9: 208–23.

one Stephano Janiculo, who aspired not merely to the throne of Moldavia, a province of Rumania, but also to the hand of Lady Arabella Stuart, herself a member of the legitimate royal family of Scotland. Somehow Stephano managed to enlist the support of two English monarchs in his extraordinary pursuit of a crown, Elizabeth recognizing his claim in 1601 (perhaps to make trouble for the Turks) and James I granting him £3000 in 1607 to forward his "restitution." His pursuit of Lady Arabella may have begun on this English visit in 1607; by 1608 he was her self-declared fiancé. In February, 1610, the English ambassador to Venice, Sir Henry Wotton, reported that on Lady Arabella's complaint a play was suppressed because it introduced an allusion to her person and to her relationship with the Prince of Moldavia. If that play was *Epicoene*, it could not have then alluded to the one time now known when Lady Arabella played an epicene part. In June, 1611, at least a year after the first production of *Epicoene*, she disguised herself as a boy to escape from the Bishop of York, who had charge of her after her secret marriage to Sir William Seymour. (Since she was connected to both the Tudor and Stuart lines, first Elizabeth, then James tried to prevent her from marrying and thus further complicating claims to the throne.) When she was "re-captured," she was imprisoned in the Tower, where she died, apparently insane, in September, 1615.

Anyone who wishes to pursue the complex questions of dating, political censorship, and Jonson's attitude toward criticism should start with Herford and Simpson's summary in 5: 144–47, and follow their references to primary sources. Note that: 1. Jonson emphasizes his innocence in his dedication to Sir Francis Stuart in which he claims that "there is not a line or syllable in it changed from the simplicity of the first copy"; 2. he wrote a second prologue, "*occasioned by some person's impertinent exception*"; 3. the title pages of both the 1616 Folio text and the 1620 Quarto edition quote lines from Horace, *Satires*, I.4.69–70 in which the author asks why one should fear him since he is no professional informer; 4. in his dedication to *Volpone* (February 11, 1607) Jonson describes the high office of the poet and scores those "*inuading interpreters*" who "*vtter their owne virulent malice vnder other mens simplest meanings*" (H & S, 5: 19); 5. the discrepancy between the first performance of *Epicoene* (early 1610) and Lady Arabella's epicene disguise (June, 1611) leads one to wonder if Jonson capitalized on contemporary gossip by later adding an allusion, or if an actor in a later performance using a

Appendix

line already there, by a particular emphasis, linked the Prince and his epicene mistress. Since Jonson had been accused of such satire before (on the Court in *Cynthia's Revels*, the law and the stage in *Poetaster*, the royal authority in *Sejanus*, and the Scots in *Eastward Ho*) and even been briefly imprisoned for the Scottish references in the last play, he was perhaps justifiably sensitive on this score—and perhaps sometimes justifiably accused.

THE TEXT

The early history of the text is not clear. The play was entered on the Stationer's Register (where publishers announced their intended publications) for John Browne and John Busby on September 20, 1610, but no text was published in that year, or at least none has ever appeared. Walter Burre acquired the rights from Browne on September 28, 1612, presumably intending to print the play that year. No 1612 Quarto exists today. Simpson thinks that, because Lady Arabella was in the Tower in 1612, Burre might have prudently given up the idea of an edition. William Gifford, whose edition of Jonson's works appeared in 1816, claims to have seen a quarto dated 1612, but no one else has. The first known text is that of the 1616 Folio. In this edition, Jonson, anxious to clear himself of charges of slandering the royal family, dedicated the play to Sir Francis Stuart and added a second prologue, criticizing those who "make a libel which he made a play." This Folio text, presumably proofread by Jonson but "not with his usual care," contains numerous misprints, several of them of importance. In 1620 William Stansby, the publisher of the Folio, reissued *Epicoene* in quarto in what Simpson calls "a grossly careless reprint of the 1616 Folio" (*H & S*, 5: 150).

Since no quarto of independent textual authority has appeared (if one ever existed) and since the Folios of 1640 and 1692 derive from the first Folio, the authoritative text of *Epicoene* must be that of the first Folio. None of the editions of *Epicoene* printed before the twentieth century is free from errors, and even the more recent Herford and Simpson *Works* is not entirely reliable so far as the text of *Epicoene* is concerned, for two reasons. First, as Johan Gerritsen argues in his study of the Folio, Simpson was wrong to conclude that the small paper sheets of gathering 2 Y (the prologues and the play up to II.2.64) were the original settings, and that the large paper sheets were careless resettings, probably by a workman who did not consult Jonson. The contrary seems true: the original setting of this gathering appears in the large paper copies (and is useful because it probably follows author's copy), and the "ordinary" copies of the small paper sheets are the resettings, and are "obviously corrected by the author."[2] L. A. Beaurline, who duplicated Gerritsen's study, agrees with this conclusion. Second, unfortunately the Herford and Simpson edition seems to have used for printer's copy the edition of Aurelia Henry (1906), at least for the last three acts. This edition, while helpful for its annotation, introduced some unique textual errors (which reappear in Herford and Simpson), such as the wrong speech prefix at IV.6.109 and the misreadings at IV.2.16 and IV.5.99. Of course these defects do not render so substantial an edition as Herford and Simpson useless, but they do require the correction they receive at the hands of L. A. Beaurline, whose reliable textual study of the play forms the basis of his excellent modern spelling edition.[3]

The present edition reprints the text as established by Herford and Simpson, with necessary corrections, but it modernizes the spelling and the punctuation. The Folio stage directions have been kept; additions to them have been enclosed in brackets.

2. Gerritsen, "Stansby and Jonson Produce a Folio: a Preliminary Account", *English Studies* 40 (1959), pp. 52–55.
3. *Epicoene, or The Silent Woman*, ed. L. A. Beaurline (Lincoln, Nebraska, 1966), pp. xix–xxiii.

Selected Reading List

EDITIONS

H and S. *Ben Jonson*, ed. C. H. Herford and Percy and Evelyn Simpson. 11
vols. Oxford, 1925–52. The standard edition. The text of *Epicoene*
appears in Volume 5, the introduction in Volume 2, and the
commentary in Volume 10.
Gifford. *The Works of Ben Jonson*, ed. William Gifford; intro. Francis Cun-
ningham. 5 vols. London, 1875.
Epicoene, or the Silent Woman, ed. Aurelia Henry. Yale Studies in English, 31.
New Haven, 1906.
Beaurline. *Epicoene, or the Silent Woman*, ed. L. A. Beaurline. Regents
Renaissance Drama Series, Lincoln, Nebraska, 1966.

CRITICISM

Barish, Jonas. *Ben Jonson and the Language of Prose Comedy*, pp. 145–86.
Cambridge, Mass., 1960.
———. "Ovid, Juvenal, and *The Silent Woman*." *PMLA* 71 (1956): 213–24.
Campbell, O. J. "The Relation of *Epicoene* to Aretino's *Il Marescalco*."*PMLA*
46 (1931): 752–62.
Donaldson, Ian. "A Martyrs Resolution: Jonson's *Epicoene*." *Review of
English Studies* 18 (1967): 1–15.
Eliot, T. S. "Ben Jonson." *Selected Essays 1917–1932*, pp. 127–39. New York,
1932.
Enck, John. *Jonson and the Comic Truth*, pp. 132–50. Madison, Wisconsin,
1957.

Selected Reading List

Heffner, Ray L. "Unifying Symbols in the Comedy of Ben Jonson." *English Stage Comedy*, ed. W. K. Wimsatt, pp. 74–97. New York, 1955.

Knoll, Robert. *Ben Jonson's Plays: an Introduction*, pp. 105–17. Lincoln, Nebraska, 1964.

Levin, Harry. Introduction to *Selected Works of Ben Jonson*. New York, 1938.

Partridge, Edward. *The Broken Compass: a study of the Major Comedies of Ben Jonson*, pp. 161–77. New York, 1958.

Salingar, L. G. "Farce and Fashion in *The Silent Woman*." *Essays and Studies by Members of the English Association* 20 (1967): 29–46.

Thayer, Calvin. *Ben Jonson: Studies in the Plays*, pp. 66–84. Norman, Oklahoma, 1963.